BRITISH SAIL

By the same author

Over Snape Bridge 1967
Woodbridge and Beyond 1972
East Coast Sail 1972
Scottish Sail 1974
North East Sail 1976

BRITISH SAIL

Robert Simper

David & Charles Newton Abbot London
North Pomfret(VT) Vancouver

To Caroline and Jonathan

ISBN 0 7153 7263 7
Library of Congress Catalog Card
Number 76-58784

© Robert Simper 1977

Set in Photon Bembo 12 on 12 point
and printed in Great Britain at the
Alden Press, Oxford for David &
Charles (Publishers) Limited Brunel
House Newton Abbot Devon

Published in the United States of
America by David & Charles Inc
North Pomfret Vermont 05053 USA

Published in Canada by Douglas
David & Charles Limited 1875 Welch
Street North Vancouver BC

Contents

1 Sail Supreme

The brig *Lyra* at the Fenland port of
Wisbech on 2 July 1856

Trading smack *Malvina* at Kildonan, Arran, 1908

Sailing ships are some of the most beautiful forms of transport ever devised. They are also a dangerous form of travel and the loss of life and hardship connected with them has been appalling. The truth about sail is that it was cruel and unrelenting and nothing was ever done easily, but at the same time it produced a stimulating way of life. In this book I am attempting to recapture the atmosphere of the final age of working sail in which everything was a combination of infinite beauty and prolonged personal hardship.

The use of sail to provide motive power at sea reached its peak late in the nineteenth century and was already waning by World War I. During the same period Britain had by far the largest tonnage of merchant shipping in the world. It was not of course just the ships of England, Scotland, Wales and Ireland which flew the Red Ensign, but all the Commonwealth countries as well. So that the sailing ships and seamen of Canada, Australia, New Zealand and South Africa, to say nothing of dozens of smaller countries and islands within the firm embrace of the British Empire, were all regarded as British. What is equally true, but more easily forgotten, is that in the Imperial age the men of numerous races, speaking a wide range of languages and dialects, were genuinely proud to sail under the Red Ensign. The term British sail could have covered a third of the world's shipping, but in this pictorial record it will be confined mainly to the British Isles, an area geographically small, but within which were dozens of coastal cultures which had their own individual types of craft.

Left on their own these coastal communities would not have progressed very far, but by joining forces the United Kingdom countries created a strong united Britain. Within this, each region retained its own strong identification, but the pooling of resources put the shipping interest in a strong position. There was however constant rivalry by other maritime nations to try to surpass Britain's domination of the world trade. The United States produced clipper ships which stole records and, more important, freights from under the noses of British owners. France strove to create an equally numerous mercantile navy, while Germany, bursting with all the energy of a new nation, built sailing ships of a very high standard; but none really ever equalled the vast fleet of British-registered sailers.

In the second half of the nineteenth century alongside the great struggle for power amongst the European nations was another battle. This was the bitter fight for sailing ships to survive against the new, cheaply built steamers. The sailing ships of the early nineteenth century all had beamy wooden hulls which rode the seas like plump ducks. They were slow, and if not overloaded were quite seaworthy. Their sail areas were small and easily controlled by a few men.

Competition with the hated steamers meant that sailing ships had to be larger and faster. The average merchant sailing vessel was still very small—the legendary *Cutty Sark* is only 963 tons gross, and for over a decade after she was built in 1869 this was about the average tonnage. The iron barque *Peru*, built on the Firth of Forth at Abden in 1873, was 710 tons gross (even smaller), yet was a successful ocean trader and for years brought her Dundee owners a steady return on their capital. She was not a clipper and spent months crossing the oceans from one port to the next, but she was a strong and comfortable ship. Eventually she was bought by John Stewart & Company, and for another twenty years she plied steadily between the United Kingdom and New Zealand.

Then she became too small for this and the barque was sold to J.J. Craig of Auckland, a general merchant who had got together the finest fleet of sailing ships in Australasia. Under the name *Louisa Craig* she was engaged solely in the inter-colonial trade between New Zealand and Australia. In the 1900s the movements of the small colonial barques were keenly followed and there was competition amongst them to make smart passages. Under another name, *Raupo*, this barque earned a good reputation until finally a slump in the Pacific freight rates led to her being sold for a coal hulk in 1921, by which time she had done forty-six years of hard ocean sailing without a serious accident.

The career of the 694-ton gross barque *Polly Woodside* is very similar. She was built by Workman, Clark & Company at Belfast in 1885 for Glasgow owners, and traded all over the world until she ran aground in New Zealand in 1903 and was sold to A.H. Turnbull. Now renamed the *Rona*, she traded in the Pacific until running ashore at Barretts Reef in the mouth of Wellington Harbour in 1921. By this time such a tiny sailer could not hope to pay for repair, let alone continue to find freights.

The *Peru* and the *Polly Woodside* belonged to the age when small cargoes were moved about the world between small ports which often had nothing more than a simple riverside quay. In the early 1880s there was tremendous expansion of trade between Britain and her fast-growing colonies, and this led to a boom for the sailing ship which loaded 1,000 tons and made long voyages by using the trade-wind systems. The profits from these small square-riggers were reinvested in new ships which, although rigged in the same way, were about twice the size. The full-rigged ship *Cambuskenneth* could load over twice as much as the beautiful little *Peru*, although both were engaged in much the same trades. By the late 1880s sailing-ship owners stopped worrying about fast passages and instead ordered even larger ships which were designed for maximum capacity, not speed. These huge sailing warehouses could often load over 4,000 tons, yet they only carried the same crews as the tiny clippers of thirty years earlier.

The barque *Louisa Craig* sailing
down Hauraki Gulf to Auckland at the
end of a voyage from Australia

The barque *Rona*, ex *Polly Woodside*,
was in the New Zealand – San
Francisco trade during World War I

The barque *Louisa Craig* sailing
down Hauraki Gulf to Auckland at the
end of a voyage from Australia

The barque *Rona*, ex *Polly Woodside*,
was in the New Zealand – San
Francisco trade during World War I

The barque *Polly Woodside* was
described as the prettiest vessel
ever launched in Belfast

The full-rigged ship *Cambuskenneth*
shortly after she was built by
Russell & Company on the Clyde in
1893

The Russell-built *Ben-Y-Gloe* wrecked on the south Glamorgan coast at the start of her maiden voyage

The *Cambuskenneth* making sail astern
a San Francisco tugboat

The barque *Alida* being built at one of
Russell & Company's Clyde yards
for Norwegian owners

Crew aloft furling the forecourse on the *Medway* in 1910

(*right*) The barque *C.B. Pedersen* being towed into the Tyne in 1928. She was one of a small fleet of Scandinavian sailing ships, mostly owned in Finland's Åland Islands, which made one voyage a year from Australia to Europe with grain

The *Glenogil* was built by Russell & Company in 1892 to join the fleet operated by J. Edgar & Company, Liverpool

Most of the huge sailers of the 1890s were the four-masted barques like *Medway* and *Glenogil*, and they were the bulk carriers on long ocean routes. To begin with these huge British barques were good money-earners and a high percentage of their earnings was ploughed back into building yet more ships. At this time Sunderland claimed to build more ships than any other town in the world. Sunderland had long been at the centre of the coal trade; not only did hundreds of colliers sail from the River Wear every year, but most of them had been built on the river. Take one year, 1869, when a total of 942 ships was launched from British yards. Of these, 124 came from yards along the first four miles of the deep but narrow River Wear. Glasgow was the nearest rival with 107, but the three main Clyde centres together produced 161.

Building demands fluctuated with the state of world trade, but the Clyde gradually became the shipbuilding centre of not just the British Empire but the whole world. In the late-Victorian and early-Edwardian eras the best-quality ships at the cheapest price were Clyde built. It was a formula which could not fail. From their three yards on the Clyde the builders Russell & Company contributed from 1885 to 1896 more sailing ships to the world's merchant fleet than any other builders.

There is a legend that Russells once had thirty new sailing ships at some point of construction all at the same time. They seem to have spent several years gradually increasing the number of ships they built, and the peak seems to have been in 1892 when the records show that they built twenty-nine new sailing ships. Yet how quickly

Furling sails on the four-masted barque
C.B. Pedersen

the peak passed, for four years later the number had dropped to only four new sailing ships in a year, and over the next decade the Clyde yards only produced the occasional barque.

Certainly by 1904 sailing ships had stopped giving reasonable returns on the capital invested, and British owners were starting to sell them off as soon as a foreign buyer could be found. By 1920 there were only a handful left and the last of these was the four-masted barque *Garthpool*. This great steel vessel had been built by W.B. Thompson of Dundee in 1891 as the *Juteopolis*. Her end came in November 1929 when on a passage from Hull to Australia she ran ashore on a Cape Verde Island reef.

2 Fishermen and Whalers

Captain David Gray and Robert Gray,
Master and mate of the Dundee
whaler *Eclipse*

Even while the barque *Eclipse* is
being forced through the ice by a hand
capstan, a man is at the mainmast
truck watching for whales

The Peterhead whaler *Eclipse* boring
through the Arctic ice floes

Most of the tiny walled-in harbours on the East Coast of
Scotland were built in the nineteenth century as bases for
the ever-expanding fishing fleets. The catching of herring
was an important form of employment along the whole of
this coast. The working life of the fisher folk was desperate
and severe, but for most there simply was no alternative.
The boats used were double ended and had two masts on
which were set huge lug sails. The two main types were
fifies on the East Coast and zulus in the Moray Firth. The
lug rig was retained because it was simple and fast. The
herrings had to be ashore and be cured within twelve
hours of being taken from the sea.

Fishing gave a living to many, but whaling brought a
fortune to a few. At one time many British ports had sent
ships into the Arctic in search of whales, but by the 1860s it
was only really Dundee, Aberdeen and Peterhead which
were seriously engaged in whaling. The voyages started in
the spring when the whalers headed north to the Shetlands
where the majority of the crew were recruited. From here
they voyaged to the whaling grounds off Greenland and
sometimes north of Russia. As the annual onslaught of
Scottish and American whalers steadily emptied the sea of
'fish' they were forced to push farther north into the
Canadian Arctic. This meant that often they could not
make a voyage in the short summer, so the whalers were
obliged to stay the winter in the Arctic and return the
following summer. In 1878, *The Perseverance*, for instance,
left Peterhead on 19 July and reached the whaling grounds
a month later, but did not see any whales before she took
up winter quarters in November.

On the 1888 voyage of *Eclipse* she carried fifty-six men. Here are some trying to wash away the smell of the whales

The Scottish whaling men took their 'fish' by harpoons fired from small, open pulling-boats

Some of the crew of *Eclipse* are curing a polar-bear skin. The whalers hunted any animal which had a saleable value

The following spring the *Perseverance* got out of the ice on 31 March, in fact earlier than normal, cruised all summer, and only took one whale before she returned to Peterhead in August. Although a successful voyage could bring wealth to all concerned with it, the number of ships declined steadily. In 1863 the seventeen Peterhead whalers returned with 18,000 seals and only fifteen whales. Six years later eight whalers went to the Greenland fishery from Peterhead and returned with 3,000 seals and six whales. In 1883 fourteen whalers sailed from Dundee and seven went from Peterhead. Most of them had by then small steam auxiliary engines to help them through the ice.

The Victorian whalers captured the 'fish' by harpoons fired from an open boat. One hunt is recorded on the barque *Perseverance* when she was sent north by the Hudson's Bay Company in 1892 to oppose the American whalers' trading activities in the Canadian Arctic. The four boats from *Perseverance* sighted a whale at 7 am, but lost it. They started chasing another whale at 6 pm and finally killed it at 8 pm, but it took until the next afternoon to tow it back and start the grisly operation of

On *Eclipse* whalebones are being cleaned. Above the men are some of the heavy blocks of the tackles used for lifting the whale carcass aboard

In the 1870s the men of Orkney earned good money working oysters, but thirty years later the Orkadians found the local stocks exhausted. In the boat is a glass-topped tunnel used to look down into the water; oysters were then picked up one by one with a long pole

flensing. In 1876 a whale taken by the *Eclipse* died at 900 fathoms and it took the whaler's crew nine hours of desperate work on the windlass to haul it back to the surface.

The Scottish whaleboats when hunting always stayed within sight of the ships and brought the whales back for flensing, while their rivals from New England established shore bases and the cutting up and flensing was done alongside the whaler. For this reason the whaler's deck was kept free from the gear needed to control the sails. The square foresail for instance was on a bentick boom, a spar at the bottom of the lowest square sail.

The Grays of Peterhead were in whaling for four generations and claimed the longest connection with it of any British family. Captain David Gray was master of the *Eclipse* from the time she was built in 1867 until 1890. His son Robert Gray was a student, but as Scottish Universities then had just one six-month term in the winter, he sailed in the summer as mate with his father. Later Dr. R.W. Gray wrote a great deal about whaling before he died at Newton Abbot in 1943. The writer Conan Doyle, when a medical student, went as surgeon on the whaler *Hope*.

The relentlessness of the Scottish and American whalers meant that by 1900 there were not enough whales left to hunt. The whaling masters had been skilful ice navigators and had sailed in waters which had not been charted; later when surveys were done they were able to name the places on the charts. The whaling ships were about twice as strongly constructed as the average merchant ship. Whaling ships were used in the explorations of both Arctic and Antarctic. The *Terra Nova* was originally a Dundee whaler, but Scott's *Discovery* was specially built at Dundee in 1901 as a research ship and was larger than a whaler—it was really a steamship with auxiliary sails.

The tiny harbour at Crail on the Fife coast gave some protection from the fury of the North Sea

3 Schooners and Trading Smacks

The trading smack *Euphemia* discharging coal at Carradale, Kintyre,
in 1910

Deck view on the barque *L'Avenir*,
Prince's Dock, Glasgow, 1935

Schooners from the Clyde traded across the Western
Ocean to Newfoundland. To cross the Atlantic these
schooners all had to be in absolutely first-class condition,
but year after year the Greenock schooners, like *Renown,
Reward* and *Regard*, made this hard voyage to collect their
cargoes of dried codfish destined for the Latin countries.
There were many other Western Ocean traders, including
Brodick Castle, Culzean Castle and, the best known,
Lochranza Castle.

The Scots appear to have dropped out of the Western
Ocean trade in the 1890s and the last is reputed to have
been the Campbeltown *Finlaggan* in 1895. This little
'ninety-niner' (ton) two-masted topsail schooner was
owned by the canny shipmaster Donald Smith. He never
carried excessive sail in strong wind so as not to cause
expensive damage. Although *Finlaggan* never broke any
records she managed every year to make two fish voyages.
First she went across to Newfoundland with salt and
returned to Italy or Greece with salted cod. Again salt was

Gabbart *Mary* off Hunter's Quay,
1883

The *Charlotte Rhodes* in the North
Channel, 1975

loaded, but this time it was taken to the Shetland or Faeroe Islands from where the schooner went to Spain with fish.

The west of Scotland and north-west English ports were the first to abandon sail in favour of the small steamers. Most of the schooners were sold to owners on the other side of the Irish Sea. At Annalong in County Down a considerable fleet was amassed, but by 1935 only the *Nellie Bywater, Lochranza Castle, Goldseeker* and *Minnie* were still trading from Annalong. The Belfast shipowners John Kelley & Co began by buying Canadian-built ships, and their fleet included the brigantines *Kelpie* and *Balmarino*, the schooner *Fellow Craft* and the 214-ton barquentine *Agnes C. James* which was the largest of their sailing ships. It was however the little port of Arklow which made such a success of operating small sailing vessels in the trade from the Mersey across to small Irish ports. They bought old schooners cheaply and worked them hard, but they looked after their ships. The schooner *Harvest King* was one of them; she was built at Runcorn in 1879 and twenty years later was bought by the Kearons of Arklow who traded her across the Irish Sea for forty years. She then went on working as a motor schooner until she was broken up with the *James Postlethwaite* in 1955, by which time all the other Arklow motor schooners were rapidly dropping out of trade.

Although the steam puffers took the trade in the Scottish Western Isles, in the Clyde the Arran smacks worked right up to World War II. In the early nineteenth century the sloop was the most common form of small trading craft in the British Isles. These single-masted gaff cutters were also known as smacks and used on passenger routes. There were weekly sailings of passenger smacks from Greenock to Belfast. An advertisement for the 'elegant smack' *Sally* in 1817 states the rules that were enforced in order to keep the cabins clean. No dogs could be taken into cabins and nor were passengers allowed to get into bed wearing boots or shoes. If clean sheets were provided then passengers had to undress and not sleep fully clothed. With food, the Greenock – Belfast passage cost £1.55, but the 'forecastle passenger' only paid 25p.

The passenger smacks on the Leith – London trade were then some of the world's fastest small ships. There was great rivalry between the Leith companies to make the fastest passage south, but the average was about five days to London. The railways and steamers quickly took over

passenger carrying, but the Orkney 'clipper' schooner *Pomona* carried passengers between Kirkwall and Leith up until 1890, while the smack *Klydon* did passenger work in the Orkney Islands for a few more years after this.

Steamers naturally took on the passenger routes in the Cyde, but on the Isle of Arran they still found smacks the most convenient form of transport. Arran is about twenty miles long and six miles across, but it has only two real harbours—at Lamlash and Lochranza. This meant that a great deal of beach work was done, and one of the places smacks brought cargoes to was The Cleits on the south-west coast of Arran. The farmers here joined together to get the coal ashore on one tide and later weighed and distributed it.

Usually Arran smacks loaded coal or building material in Ardrossan, Irvine, Troon and Ayr, and then sailed to one of the islands in the Clyde or a landing place on Kintyre. In *Scottish Sail* I have recorded more of the Arran smacks and that the best ones were built by William Fife & Son, Fairlie. The *Retriever*, 1874, *Jessie Kerr*, 1880, and the *Mary Kerr*, 1884, were notable, but the last smack launched was the *Betsy Crawford* at Ardrossan in 1902. In the Clyde there were also double-ended, round-bottomed barges known as gabbarts. Really intended for work through the Forth and Clyde Canal, they had a simple gaff-sloop rig but the gabbarts did not sail as well as the smacks. One trader of the gabbart type was the *Catharine McColl*, owned by Campbell of Ardrishaig, which had a 50ft-long main boom and a round stern and blunt bow. Nothing would induce her to go to windward properly.

Before being confined to the Clyde, smacks had worked to all the Western Isles. The Highlanders used to come south by smack in search of summer work in the lowlands. The Arran smack *Duchess* was for a time owned on Lismore, an island farther north in Loch Linnhe. I thought of the seamen of Lismore in the September of 1975 while passing the low green island in the three-masted topsail schooner *Charlotte Rhodes*. We had come from Inverness through the Caledonian Canal to arrive at the Corpach locks in what appeared to be almost hurricane conditions, with a screaming gale driving endless rain. We had waited, hoping the autumn gales would blow themselves out, and then we tried to snatch a passage to Swansea. The sail-training topsail schooner *Captain Scott* came in from the sea, keeping under the lee of the towering cliffs of

Mull. In the winter sometimes she is forced to ride out gales in the lochs with both anchors down and engines running and still only just managing to hold her position.

For the tiny smacks, ketches and schooners which once brought Ayrshire coal round Kintyre to the Western Isles, life must have been very difficult. Bound north, the traders used to go through the Sound of Islay to avoid the infamous Corryvreckan tidal race. Even the narrow passage between Islay and Jura had a nasty race when a strong southerly wind blew over the ebb. The wooden topsail schooner *Mary Stewart* was once bound for Tiree with coal when she hit bad conditions at the southern end of the Sound of Islay. Fortunately, being in good order, she survived although her bulwarks were washed away by the seas.

Being aware of these conditions the *Charlotte Rhodes* avoided the island passages and stood out past Colonsay. Huge dark-blue seas rolled in to burst on the outlying solid grey rocks of Colonsay in a mass of boiling white surf. It was here that the little Inverness-built schooner *Senator* came to an end in 1887. She was beating past the island but missed stays and went to pieces on a Colonsay reef. That evening on the *Charlotte Rhodes* a watery sun broke through and behind Islay we could see a rain shower passing over the far-away hills.

The wind remained fresh and by the following mid-day we had passed through the North Channel. But then it was obvious that another gale was coming and we turned back, hoping to make Stranraer. Rapidly the wind increased to north-east, force 10. The *Charlotte Rhodes* had been built in Denmark in 1903 and had traded across the North Atlantic for her first twenty years. Under mizzen, gaff foresail and inner jibs she took it all in her stride, but a depressing amount of water swilling wildly about in the main hold began to increase. It appeared that some of the caulking between the planks was working loose as the hull ploughed through the gale-lashed sea.

The crew of four began a long stint of pumping and bailing; I did relief spells on the wheel while the captain tried to make radio contact with any ship in the area. For about four hours the *Charlotte Rhodes* had to battle alone against the fury of the Irish Sea, then between heavy rain showers we saw the coast of Northern Ireland. For us it was a lee shore and with darkness approaching this placed the schooner in an uncomfortable situation. The Captain's request for assistance was picked up by a new Belfast supertanker and they fixed our position. Shortly after, the Donaghadee lifeboat came out and the coxwain gave advice over the radio on the course into Belfast Lough.

Once under the shelter of the land the *Charlotte Rhodes* was not hard pressed and the port-side leak stopped. Going up to our berth in the troubled city of Belfast we passed the *Result*, which had been built as a schooner on Belfast Lough at Carrickfergus in 1893. Two schooners together, survivors of another and very different age.

4 Ocean and Coastal Schooners

The 37-ton *Petrel* was only the size
of a trading smack, but was given
the topsail-schooner rig so beloved
by British coasting men

Liverpool and the Mersey was the centre of trade in the Irish Sea. The shipping interests of Liverpool were devoted to international trade and ships left the Mersey for every corner of the globe. To the hundreds of small sailing-ship owners all round the Irish Sea, Liverpool was the place they collected freights from but did not belong to. The small rural schooner ports supplied the raw materials for the huge industrial centres of population in north-west England. In turn the schooners returned back to their home ports with imported or manufactured goods. For instance the Solway Firth schooners took granite south and returned with imported cattle food.

The steady expansion of industry in the nineteenth century created new ports such as Connah's Quay on the River Dee, which was an outlet for bricks and tiles going to Belfast and Dublin. The capital this trade created led to the building up of a considerable fleet of schooners, many of them built at Connah's Quay by Ferguson & Baird. The *Windermere* and *Kathleen & May* are the best known of their schooners, but they also turned out a number of 'Earl' schooners for various members of the Raynes family of Abergale. This ended with the last schooner built here, the *Earl of Beaconsfield*, in 1903.

The topsail schooner *James Postlethwaite*, built by Thomas Ashburner & Sons at Barrow in 1881, carried the sail-plan that Victorian seamen found the most practical for a small sailing ship. With all her lower sails fore and aft this meant she was easy to handle, while the square topsails on the foremast gave a real driving force, far more than the gaff topsails of the coasting ketch. When coming about on a fresh tack the square topsails abacked first and pushed the head round. With their many sails of a small area schooners very rarely had to go to the laborious and dangerous operation of reefing in a gale; they simply took in another sail. The ketch rig only became practical in larger vessels when small auxiliaries were fitted, because although this sail-plan required less work than the schooner, it was not as effective.

The *James Postlethwaite* had square topsails typical of those used in the British coasting trade. The great drawback was that to stow them a hand had to go aloft on to the yards. Another method, used on the French schooners, was to have a single square sail which was rolled around the yard. This was done from the deck so that no one went aloft; also as the wind increased the sail

The *Ocean Gem* of Dumfries in the River Nith off Glencaple. She was built as a fishing boat, but later cut in half and lengthened, and she lasted until 1939

could be rolled down as a form of reefing. The roller topsail was a slightly more versatile sail, but it too had disadvantages. There was heavy chain aloft, and the general friction on the sails and gear was a constant problem. Much has been written about how superior the roller topsail was over the British method, but in practice it seems that both methods had advantages and drawbacks. It is significant that several Moray Firth schooners were built with roller topsails, but soon reverted to the normal type.

In the industrial world of the Victorian era the schooner was simply the most reliable form of transport for the middle-range freight tonnage. Schooners were used by the newly developed mining companies on the Cumbrian coast to move iron ore to South Wales. On the Duddon Estuary two rival companies began shipping ore out from two separate piers. At a meeting in 1866 it was decided to call this port Millom. However, the decision was far from unanimous and one company continued to call it Duddon.

The Danish schooner *Rise* was the last trader to leave the River Nith solely under canvas when she sailed from Dumfries for Fowey in March 1924. The tidal conditions in the Solway Firth were difficult and the first auxiliary was fitted to the *North Barrule* at Kippford in 1909

The *Petrel* discharging coal on the open Solway beach at Carsethorn in the early 1920s. She was the smallest British schooner, but little was known of her origin until she was broken up. Then they found she had been built at Liverpool in 1852

The first schooner built here was registered as being built at Millom, but on her stern was carved *Nellie Bywater* of Duddon, Port of Whitehaven.

Millom was an exacting place to load because it dried out at low water and this threw tremendous strain on the wooden-hulled schooners. Yet the *Nellie Bywater* was in this trade for forty years before she was sold away from Millom. Most schooners had their square sails removed when auxiliaries were installed but the *Nellie Bywater* was the last topsail schooner on the British register when she was lost in 1952. The last trader built at Millom (and in the British Isles) was the *Emily Barratt*, in 1913. She started as a topsail schooner, but when sold to Portmadoc owners in 1922 was converted to an auxiliary ketch.

The man who built the *Nellie Bywater* in 1873 was William Thomas who, like his yard foreman Hugh Jones, came from Amlwch on Anglesey. There was a strong

Swansea schooner *CWA Avon* and the Norwegian brig *Ernst & Maria* at Douglas, Isle of Man

Dublin trading smack *Ariel* and a
topsail schooner at Ramsey, Isle of
Man

Flax and canvas sails soon turn to
mildew if stowed wet. Here traders
are drying sails at Ramsey, Isle of Man

Fleetwood trawlers favoured a very
square-cut topsail *Harriet* (right)

connection between Anglesey and the Cumbrian mining
ports. William Thomas had a yard in both places and in
his Amlwch yard he built the *Cumberland Lassie*, 1878, and
the *Kate*, both for Cumberland mining interests.

Ownership shares of the schooners in the ore and
general trades were spread widely between men connected
with mine management and the individual miners.
William Thomas, the shipbuilder, worked closely with

William Postlethwaite of Millom, who had built up a
large interest in local mining and shipping.

Most of the coastal trade on this coast was of course
from the Mersey and the Dee. When a stiff south-westerly
wind barred their passage across the Irish Sea the ketches
and schooners sailed down under the lee of the North
Wales hills and anchored under the shelter of Anglesey in
Moelfre Bay. If the wind went round to the north-east

Even in the 1950s a few Arklow-
owned motor schooners like the
Windermere were trading across the
Irish Sea with coal from the Mersey

then Moelfre Bay quickly turned into a death trap. Before World War I it was quite common to see around seventy sailing vessels caught here. It was impossible to beat out, so they kept plunging up and down in the heavy seas. With all these sailing traders the huge windlass and powerful bow was an obvious feature, because they spent far more time riding at their anchors windbound than underway sailing. The force of the bows of the schooner lifting up and snatching at the anchor chain was enormous. At any time the cable could part or the windlass be torn bodily from the bows.

At Moelfre the sailing lifeboat was often out all night, beating about in a gale, taking out spare anchors and picking up the crews of vessels which were going to be driven ashore. To the people of Moelfre a shipwreck was something of a blessing. One schooner came ashore near

The *Windermere* was laid up at Arklow in 1956 after damage received when she ran aground on the Tusker Rock, near Porthcawl. The winch-house just aft of the foremast was added to many British, Irish and Baltic schooners

The topsail schooner *James Postlethwaite* was sold across the Irish Sea to Arklow owners and spent World War I interned at Hamburg

the lifeboat shed and within a week there was not a trace of the 200 tons of coal she had been carrying.

Some of the tiles which the *Ellen Harris* was carrying when she was lost on Moelfre Island in 1915 were still to be found half a century later. She had come out of the Dee, probably loaded incorrectly, which had spoilt her sailing trim. Anyway, it was a fine day with a good breeze, but the crew just could not get the *Ellen Harris* to come about and she just ploughed into the rocks.

Even the subsidence of a gale brought little aid for the schooner men. Usually the wind dropped away completely and the vessels had to be kedged clear of the land so that the tide could sweep them out into the Irish Sea. Some of the crew would row ahead and drop another anchor on 120 fathoms of rope. The other members of the crew then hauled the schooner up to this anchor. While they were doing this the men in the boat would be rowing out with a second anchor. Slowly, very slowly the schooner would creep out to sea.

The last schooners owned on this coast belonged to Clark & Grounds of Runcorn. One of the Upper Mersey

The *Emily Barratt* was bought by
George Welch of Braunton, North
Devon, in 1928

In the River Mersey and connecting
waterways freight was moved in
sloop-rigged barges called Mersey
Flats

This Mersey Flat shows a great similarity to the Clyde gabbarts

The topsail schooner waiting her turn to load slate at Port Dinorwic has her square topsail hanging loose in the gaskets so that the yards may be painted

traders was the three-master *Mary Miller*, and her passages show how unpredictable sail could be. She was once seven days on passage from Plymouth to Goole, but another time she took thirty-seven days on the same trip. The Lancashire schooner *Happy Harry* was fifty-five days going between Shoreham and Llanelly. But an even longer voyage lasting all winter was once made by a Runcorn schooner in the regular Cornish china-clay trade. She left the Mersey in early October, but the mother of one of her seamen had to post a cake down to them in Charlestown where they only arrived in time for Christmas.

As well as being the port of
registration for many North Wales
schooners, Caernarvon had a
thriving coastal trade

A topsail schooner, with a pointed
Irish Sea stern, sails into the
Beaumaris end of the Menai Straits,
1902

The three-masted topsail schooner
Cumberland Lassie was built at the
tiny copper-mine port of Amlwch and
was wrecked in January 1918

Crew of the *John Pritchard*. 'Jack
Klondyke' Williams with hand on
wheel, William and Rhys Lloyd and,
in front, William Watkin Roberts and
the boy David Nicholas

The steel schooner *Mary B. Mitchell*
at Preston. She was built at
Carrickfergus in 1892 and traded
with slate from Port Penrhyn. After
a successful spell as a Q Ship in
World War I she was sold to Tyrell
of Arklow. Finally wrecked in the
Solway Firth in 1944

The *Kate* was built at Graves, Isle of Man, in 1872 and was the last schooner owned at Amlwch when she was lost by fire off Moelfre in 1933

5 Slate Traders and more Schooners

The schooner *Dovey Belle* at Aberdovey where she was built by Thomas Richards in 1867. Spritsail boats like the one in the foreground seem to have been widely used in Cardigan Bay

The *Dalgonar* docking at Liverpool
after arriving from Australia

The towns and villages around Cardigan Bay were in effect cut off from the inland district by the Cambrian Mountains. Since travel by land was difficult they looked to the sea to link them with the world outside, so there grew up a strong tradition of going to sea in small sailing ships. Although Welsh sailors took to the sea as their second home, the ports they originated from still remained isolated communities with fierce local pride. This social background produced men of stubborn tenacity, which was the very quality needed to persuade a sailing vessel from one port to the next. The Welshmen went to sea because they had to, but when they got there they were capable seamen.

The sense of isolation from the rest of Europe was weakened by the great slate boom of the second half of the nineteenth century. Other minerals were mined too, but it was the need for cheap roofing material which created prosperity for the smaller ports. The merchants here had always been able to exploit the continental market. There is a legend that Barmouth received its English name just so that merchants in the buying ports could pronounce it, and more important, distinguish it from the other rival Welsh ports. Another new port, Portmadoc, also took a name which fitted easily into the far-away builders-merchants' ledgers, but the quarries of Snowdonia poured out slate in such vast quantities that soon the Portmadoc schooners became well known throughout the western world.

Shipowners took pride in giving their vessels an English

The launching of *Gestiana* at Portmadoc in 1913 for the Newfoundland trade

name so that they were easily identified as part of Britannia's mighty merchant fleet, but these tightly knit communities were very reluctant to let any monetary gain stray far from the land of its origin. Welsh slate went into Welsh-owned schooners which were sailed by Welsh-speaking crews. Yet strangely there was really nothing particularly Welsh about the ships that the slate trade produced, but they were some of the best small sailing ships built anywhere. At the beginning of the slate trade most of the Cardigan Bay vessels were brigs such as were common in all British ports. Then, following the pattern of development which evolved in the ports of North and West Britain, the schooner became almost unrivalled by the 1870s. By this time Portmadoc was not only sending

slate to most northern-European ports, but had branched out into other trades, particularly into the taking of dry cod from Newfoundland across to the Latin countries. In fact they specialised in taking small freights across the oceans. The West Country and some Clyde schooners were doing the same work, but Portmadoc really evolved a highly successful vessel for this work in the three-masted, standing-topgallant yard schooner. It made the best use of all the nineteenth-century sailing-ship technology in having three main lower gaff sails which allowed the vessel to point fairly close to the wind and was economical in requiring a small crew to handle them. On the foremast were three square sails which gave tremendous pulling power, especially on down-wind sailing.

The *Ellen Beatrice* at the Aberdovey
Pier. She was built at Aberystwyth
by Evans in 1865

The brig *Sir Robert McClure* on the
stocks at Aberystwyth

The *City of Birmingham* was one of
the Aberystwyth pleasure boats.
They were specially designed for the
steep beach and had standing-gaff
sails. This one became a fishing
boat at Conway

Another feature of these schooners was the powerful
clipper bow and deep foot which they needed, because,
with so much sail forward, they had to be able to grip the
water under the bow. The *Gestiana* had this high-shaped
bow which could plough through the seas. The later
Newfoundland traders were very superior vessels to the
usual small coasting schooners. I knew an old schooner-
hand who called them Western Ocean Yachts because
they were so smart and made fast Atlantic passages.

Eventually the railway came pushing through the
mountains and soon slate was being moved away by land.
The little port of Portmadoc did all it could to compete.
The slate wharves were roofed in so that the rain did not
slow up work, and two tugs speeded the slate traders into

The Llangranog regular traders: ketch
Margaret Ellen, smack *Albatross*
and ketch *Eliza Jane*

the River Glaslyn. But still they could not compete with
the railways and steamers. With the slate trade failing the
owners kept their schooners in the Western Ocean trades,
but even before World War I the need for small ocean
freight-carriers was also failing. Over 200 small wooden
sailing ships were built at Portmadoc, mostly for local
owners, yet the strong sense of local independence which

had been the port's greatest asset now became its weakness.
Like many small shipping communities they kept
everything amongst themselves, including insurance. The
slate trade returns were already falling when disaster
struck. The brand new schooner *Gestiana* was lost on a
Canadian coastal passage and the financial repercussions
turned Portmadoc into just a ghost port within a decade.

The trading smack *Kate* leaving
Newport, Pembrokeshire, about 1880

The same pattern of events had happened at Aberdovey, although on a smaller scale. There had been copper and lead mining and then slate from Mid-Wales to be shipped out from the quay at the entrance of the broad, shallow River Dovey. Shipbuilding prospered alongside the trade; nothing on a grand scale, but topsail schooners like the *Dovey Belle*, which Thomas Richards built here in 1867. Some forty-five ships were built on the north bank of the Dovey, but this ended with the *Olive Branch* in 1880. Although there were foreign, Irish and coastal freights, the port was only a minor one after the local slate quarry failed.

Aberystwyth and the surrounding countryside had a large enough population to support a sizeable fleet of merchant sail. Wooden barques, brigs and schooners were built at the bend of the river below the bridge at a spot known as the Gap. Aberystwyth also had fishing ketches, as well as nobbies—which were bought from the north. The spritsail rig seems to have been widely used in Cardigan Bay, although two pleasure boats with standing gaffs were specially built to run trips off the steep beach at Aberystwyth. One of these, the *City of Birmingham*, was sold for use as a fishing boat during World War I.

Following the sweep of Cardigan Bay south, Aberayron and New Quay were also flourishing ports. As in the hill districts of North Wales, men went away to sea in large numbers from this coast. When the Cardigan Bay schooner numbers dwindled they travelled to Liverpool, London and the Welsh coal ports to join ships there. So many men were at sea that the promotion lists of the large shipping companies were put up in the barbers' shops in Aberdovey, Aberystwyth and Aberayron so that everyone could see how their neighbours were progressing.

The River Teifi at Cardigan is very shallow, and often timber, coal and livestock were discharged at St Dogmaels. With only twelve feet in the channel, schooners could only get up to Cardigan's three quays on spring tides. These difficulties seem to have encouraged the amount of beach work. At Llangranog three traders, owned in the village, unloaded coal on the open beach all through the summer, and in the winter they were laid up in the River Teifi, an unusual practice. Their way of getting the coal out was also fairly unique. A spar was hoisted aloft and a basket in the hold was fixed to the end tilted down. From the high end a rope ran down through a block fixed in the sand and then to a horse. When the horse walked forward the coal-filled basket was brought up to deck level and tipped into a cart at the side. At the same time sand was loaded as ballast for the return passage.

Farther south at Newport, Pembrokeshire, there was another little maritime trading community centred on the little quay at Parrog Bach. Really this was just a sandy expanse at the head of the bay, and the channel was so narrow that traders had to be kedged in against a head wind. On Parrog Bach there was a warehouse, three lime kilns and a sailmaker. There was also a little shipbuilding, as a local master mariner, Jacob Beer, bought up *New Providence, Newlands, Thomas & Ann* and *Crystal*—all old vessels which he had rebuilt here.

In 1884 Customs Officer Morris recorded sixty-four vessels entering Newport. The regular traders were *Speedwell, Mary Ann, Margaret Ellen* and *Kate.* Mostly they came with clum, an anthracite dust from the Pembrokeshire coalfields which was mixed with clay to form household fuel.

6 Mineral Carriers, Fishing and Pilot Skiffs

The term smack comes from a
Dutch word meaning single-masted
craft. Some of the Brixham trawlers
here off Tenby in 1884 are single-
masted cutters, but most are
ketches, the next development

The south-west corner of Wales has a coastline of tiny bays and inlets, with Milford Haven pushing far inland right up to Haverfordwest. The countryside has good farmland; this gave work in the past to numerous small ketches and smacks which moved small farm freights off the beaches. Moreover the acid soils of Pembrokeshire needed lime constantly. To get this lime, kilns were set up at most sheltered landing places so that coal could be brought in cheaply from the sea. Since all land transport was then geared to the horse and the roads were just tracks, small sailing vessels could move bulky goods very much more cheaply.

This beach work was increasingly difficult as the coast was open to the full force of the Atlantic gales. One of the worst places to get into was Porth-gain, which was not much more than a crack in the cliffs. The high ground blanketed the wind yet, with the huge swell boiling up on the rocks, the schooners had to creep in up to the tiny harbour. A rock-crushing plant was established at Porth-gain in 1878 and after this there was regular trade. In 1902, and again two years later, the harbour was improved and in just one summer, 1909, 12,000 tons of Porth-gain stone was exported and 230 tons of bricks.

Most of the trade in this corner of Wales was across the Severn Sea to Bristol and the West-Country ports. The link between the two sides of the Bristol Channel was very strong, the sea was not a barrier, but a common bond. In both Pembrokeshire and Devon small sailing ships thrived. When Captain John Russan, of Dale, Milford Haven, wanted a new ship in 1909, he bought the ketch *Garlandstone* from her Devon builder and for her first freight sailed to Portmadoc to pick up slate. For the little ketch *Isabel* built at Pembroke Dock in 1897 it was the other way round. She did beach work taking coal to Little Haven, but she and the *Garlandstone* later became hard-bitten north Devon auxiliary sailers which went on grinding out a living for decades after the lofty deep-water schooners of Portmadoc and of James Fisher & Sons of Barrow had departed from the seas. Back in 1884 Fishers had forty sailing ships, mostly in the ore trade.

It was the smelting and refining of copper at Swansea which brought about one of the toughest trades small sailing ships were ever involved in. To begin with, copper came from Cornwall, Cumberland and Anglesey, but as one source was worked out ships had to go farther afield.

What a sight! The Brixham fleet
with the old Dartmouth registration
making sail off Tenby, 1884

The Milford trawler *Willie* was first rigged as a cutter but in 1901 was altered to a ketch because smaller sails were easier to control

(*right*) This is the Tenby lugger *La Mascotte*. There seem to have been four of these earning a living taking summer trips and going after bass during the winter 'behind the Island' (Caldy)

With Tenby's strong connection with the West Country it is not surprising that most local boats were built 'over the side'. Here at Tenby in 1936 are the *Myhew, Mary, Pretty Polly* and *Two Brothers* Only the open boat *Orion*, just under the bowsprit of *Pretty Polly*, was left at Tenby in 1975

The Mumbles oyster skiffs are manoeuvring at the start of their annual race in 1922. The foreshore is covered with ballast from the French ships which once came to load iron ore from a small mine

The Mumbles skiffs *Snake* and
Hawk. These skiffs were built in
Devon on the Essex smack lines
and worked in Swansea Bay until
1930, but forty-five years later it was
still possible to trace their hulks on
Mumbles foreshore

Finally this meant round Cape Horn to the west coast of
South America. The point about the Swansea Copper-Ore
Cape Horners was that they were quite small wooden
ships, 400-600 tons, and every voyage meant rounding
Cape Horn twice. The brig *L'Esperance* looked quite
sizeable as she was towed out of Swansea bound for a
Chilean port, but later, when this deeply laden ship came
to battle against the gales and huge seas off Cape Horn, she
would have been continually awash and very much on her
own.

It was not just strong local contacts that gave the
Swansea ships a monopoly of the copper trade; their real

The Mumbles dredging skiffs are covered in lime and tallow while laid up in the Horsepool. This pool was filled in 1892 by the Railway Company who replaced it with a breakwater which proved inadequate and was swept away. This left the oystermen with no shelter for their boats

key to success was that they alone knew how to load ore. For its volume ore was exceptionally heavy, and instead of the ore being loaded straight on to the hold bottom, a trunk layout was evolved. By placing the load centrally and higher in the hold she rode easier in a seaway and did not labour. As well as this the copper-ore traders were very strongly built, mainly of greenheart or oak, and were copper fastened. Burgess & Company, the leading Swansea owners, used to have their ships built at Barnstaple and taken over to Swansea for completion.

At the height of the copper-ore trade in the 1870s Burgess owned twenty-two ships. This was not the only

The barquentine *Hilda* was built at Appledore in 1879 and was yet another sailer to be run down and sunk by a trawler in the North Sea

(*right*) The ketch *Kate* of Gloucester was on passage from Plymouth to Goole when she put into Dover with sails blown away. Next she got ashore on the Scroby Sands and was towed into Yarmouth. Finally she made Goole and then Hull, but when she returned down channel more sails were lost and she was towed into Shoreham

firm engaged in this lucrative work of feeding the smelting plants. The work created and maintained for over half a century a thriving fleet of small, deep-water sailing ships, but it finally came to an end about the time the Panama Canal was opened. Strangely, few Swansea shipowners ever went in for shipbuilding or operating steamers, nor surprisingly did any other South Wales owners. After all, coal, and particularly Welsh steam coal, was then the source of energy for the Industrial Revolution, but the competition between the collieries and shipping companies to win the foreign contracts was very cut-throat. Dealings on the Cardiff Coal Exchange were so competitive in the 1880s that a farthing (fraction of a penny) cut off the price of a ton of coal could win a contract. Best Welsh steam coal was needed wherever steam engines ran, particularly railways. Naturally every European shipowner sought to get a coal charter for an outward-bound cargo. Coal was

The *Mary Stewart* and *Eilian* at Ilfracombe in 1956. The *Eilian* was built at Amlwch in 1908 and in 1975 was still trading as a motor-ship in Denmark. The Dutch-built *De Wadden* was in the Clyde in 1975 while the wooden Runcorn schooner *Snowflake* was still working in Yugoslavia

The pilot skiffs racing from Cardiff to Lynmouth in 1903. The port authorities responsible for granting the pilot licences held an annual craft inspection, and usually after this there were keenly contested races.

The Barry skiff *Kindly Light* has her jib aback and is about to put a pilot on a small steamer. Like many of the better Bristol Channel pilot cutters she was sold for a yacht and became *Theodora.* She has since been restored at Cardiff

an intricate part of international trade and, by providing an outward freight, the cost of importing raw materials was kept down. The ruthless but efficient economic rule of the survival of the fittest in the nineteenth century created the wealth which later allowed the easier working conditions in Western Society.

The coasting schooners loaded from the smaller collieries. In Pembroke special double-ended barges brought coal down from the River Cleddau collieries. After its completion in 1849, Saundersfoot harbour was an outlet for more coal; while the transport of coal from inland, up the River Severn, from Lydney to Ireland and the West Country, was the mainstay of economy for the motor schooners and ketches owned in Appledore and Braunton right up to the end of the 1950s.

It was the world's appetite for steam coal which caused the evolution of the Bristol Channel pilot cutters. Every sizeable ship needed a pilot to enter and leave port. The pilots all operated independently and went out searching for incoming vessels. Once aboard a ship, the two pilot's men then sailed their cutter back. These gaff cutters, which they called skiffs, had to be able to stay at sea and survive in the worst winter's gale. The competition amongst pilots for the fastest and most seaworthy skiffs produced some of the world's finest small craft of the sailing-ship era.

The pilot skiffs for Barry, Cardiff and Newport racing at Cardiff in 1906. There was never any standardisation with pilot cutters, but most had low sail-plans with square mainsails which were reckoned to reduce rolling in the long Atlantic seas

All the pilot skiffs, like Barry 22, had their masts stepped relatively far aft. The pilot's man is sculling over the stern, a method of propelling small craft on windless days before engines evolved

The Bristol pilot skiffs *EMC* and *Pet* at the pilot village of Pill on the River Avon in 1937. The *Pet* was built by Cooper at Pill in 1907 for a Newport pilot. These skiffs have wonderful open decks for working on, and when at sea they carried their boats on the port deck

Norwegian barque *Gunvoy* wrecked
on the Lizard, 1913

7 Trawlers, Luggers and Oyster Boats

The single-topsail schooner
Lafrowda of Penzance in Mount's
Bay

A transom-sterned East Cornish
lugger registered at Fowey

After about 1880 the large square-rigged ships were developed to use the trade winds to make long ocean voyages. With the wind from behind, the square sails developed great driving power. However, beating against the wind was a different matter as the yards could not be braced round far enough to allow the vessel to point close to the wind. Deep-water sailing ships carried very limited navigational aids; often the master had only a rather general idea of the ship's position, so that as they closed with the land they were extremely vulnerable, particularly if confronted with poor visibility.

Cornwall was the first solid land on the fringe of the Atlantic and hundreds of sailing ships literally ploughed into it with fatal consequences. For the coasting traders bound with coal, slate and any other bulk cargo from the Western ports of Britain, the long cliff-faced Cornish peninsula had to be rounded to reach the Channel, North Sea and Continental ports. The topsail schooner *Enterprise*, built by Gough at Bridgwater in 1875, was just one of hundreds of coastal traders which found herself caught on a lee shore when she was driven ashore near St Ives in September 1903. Like most schooners of her size she had a crew of four and they were taken off by the lifeboat.

Conditions in Cornwall meant that local traders only needed to carry relatively small cargoes, but even on short passages they had to contend with oceanic conditions. The

Pilchard drivers leaving St Ives. On the right is the 34ft *Lucent* which was built on the beach at St Ives in six weeks in 1896 for £60

(*right*) The *Doris* of Salcombe. She is similar to the earlier fruit schooners

were the Truro River Oyster Boats which worked in Carrick Roads and the creeks inland of Falmouth. At the bottom of the licence which the Truro City Council issues for dredging in this oyster fishery is written 'Boats propelled by mechanical power not licenced'. These seven words create the only sailing fishing fleet left working in Northern Europe.

The actual number of boats has always fluctuated with the demand for oysters. The boats dating back to Victorian times are often as 'deep as a mine shaft', like *Mildred*, which drew over 6ft on a 28ft length, and it is probable that they were intended to go after mackerel to the Eddystone and down west to Mount's Bay when dredging was poor. These deep sail boats were faster, but the usual 4ft 6in draft was the limit so that they could remain working on the banks at low water. The sail boats were developed to be worked single handed, because in pre-World War I days men had large families and the returns from oystering were small.

Although all the creeks off Carrick Roads and the Truro River had oyster boats, Pill used to be the centre. In 1918 there were twenty-eight sail boats and about fifty haul-tow punts here and it is said that one could walk across Pill Creek on them. In the summer the men went away as yacht hands or in merchant ships and returned to fit out their boats for a hard winter's dredging. They started the season in punts. The upper Truro River men, known as 'Combe Gaffers', used to come down-river in punts with tiny lug mizzens. Some men worked just hand punts, because they were cheap to operate, but most later shifted their dredges into the sail boats. In the inter-war years a man could dredge all winter and still not be sure of selling his oysters when the French ketch called. It is hardly surprising that they would not go out in very strong winds because any damage bit deeply into their income.

Most sail boats were built on the river, but it was often cheaper to buy an old boat from outside Falmouth and adapt her. The *George Glasson* was probably built in about 1880, but was bought in 1904 by the Laitys of Flushing for oystering. The *Swallow*, which Jim Green worked for over fifty years, was a Mevagissey lugger which had been given a new bow in about 1900. In the 1930s the *May Flower* was bought from Mount's Bay, while John Merifield bought the *Endeavour* from Mousehole for about £20 at the same time.

Cornish schooners' hulls were deep and shapely with high bulwarks and the powerful, two-masted, topsail schooner sail-plan such as the *Lafrowda* was given when she was built at Plymouth in 1867. The *Doris* was built at Salcombe in 1880 and sailed for forty years as a topsail schooner, but like many others she was later cut down to a ketch to save hands. The *Katie*, built at Padstow in 1881, remained Cornish and a schooner right up to 1940 when she was the last West-Country trader to work under sail only.

With its small population the Cornish merchant sail was limited, but every port, creek or cove had a fishing fleet and at each place an individual type of craft evolved to suit local conditions. Although the St Ives luggers, Polperro gaffers, and the Brixham trawlers were well known in their day, one type remained in the background. These

The *Katie* at Polruan on the Fowey River in the 1930s. Sadly, she sank in 1972 during an attempt to bring her back from Denmark for restoration

Plymouth trawlers being given a tow
clear of the quay, 1928

The fishing boats of Polperro were
known as Gaffers

Both Brixham and Lowestoft had
sailing trawlers until World War II.
Here is the Brixham trawler *Abiah*
at Newlyn

The Plymouth Hookers, like Polperro Gaffers, had loose-footed mainsails, and the secret of this type of gaff sail was to have a long gaff. These hookers, like most small craft, had their bowsprits run in while in port

Henry Merifield dredging with the *Endeavour*, 1974. Truro River work boats are allowed to use engines to reach the banks, but never for dredging

The haul-tow punts are worked by
dropping an anchor and then drifting
back. Next a single dredge is
dropped and, with a winch in the bow,
hauled back over the anchor.

Leila dredging, 1974. She is the only
Cornish oyster boat to have been
directly influenced by the Itchen Ferry
hull shape

After World War II the oystermen believed that the fishery would fade away as they died, but then came the severe winter of 1963 which killed many oysters on the East Coast and resulted in a good demand for the Fal natives. One of the first new boats was the *Leila* which Mike Parsons built himself after his first boat, *Thelma*, was wrecked after breaking loose from her mooring at Mylor. During a gale in 1968 the *Six Brothers* broke loose from her mooring at Mylor and by the light of car headlights the men watched helplessly as she was hammered to pieces on the rocks. George Vinnicombe, who had worked her for years, had plans drawn up from the wreckage and a new *Six Brothers* was built at Plymouth in 1969.

It was the revival of Fal oyster prices in the 1960s which gave younger work-boat men confidence to start ordering new boats. Terry Heard, a former oysterman, has built most of these at his Mylor Bridge Yard. His first was the *Result*, rather a narrow boat as she was built in a garage. Next was the 22ft *Crystal Spring* in 1965 and then the Percy

The *George Glasson* follows the normal practice of dropping the staysail and using the jib to balance the main as she drifts along the oyster banks, 1974

Dalton-designed *St Meloris* in 1968. She was given the keel of the 28ft *Harriet*, a famous old oyster boat which was built by Ferris at least a century before. The *St Meloris* became the first Falmouth work boat to be sailed single handed across the Atlantic when John Jackson sailed her to Antigua. In 1970 Terry Heard built his last wooden-hulled oyster boat the *Mirre* before starting a series of fibreglass hulls based on the lines of *St Meloris*. First the *Meloris* in 1972, then the *Three Sisters* in 1973 for John Wallis, then the *Helen Mary* and *Kindly Light* for John Moon in 1974.

In the autumn of 1974 there were forty-four working boats in the Falmouth area, but many were yachts and only nineteen were in commission dredging. They were: from Mylor: 28ft *Six Brothers*, 24ft *Caterina*, 27ft *Evaline*, 27ft *Shadow*, 24ft *Leila*, 28ft *Three Sisters*, 28ft *Kindly Light*; from Falmouth-Flushing: 30ft *George Glasson*, 24ft 8in *Beatrice*, 22ft *Mirre*, 27ft *Result*, 28ft *Helen Mary*; from Restronguet: 32ft *Morning Star*, 24ft 8in *Five Sisters*, 25ft 6in *Stella*; from Pill: 27ft *Endeavour*, 25ft *Muriel*, 25ft *Ivy*; and from Truro River: 21ft *Julie*.

The work-boat men approached summer racing with the same competitive air of professionalism as winter dredging. The races start in June and continue every Saturday for the rest of the summer. Only the fast boats race regularly and in the 1960s the old *Six Brothers*, *Victory*, *Florence* and *George Glasson* were considered the fastest, but competition to produce a prize-winning boat is very keen. Topsails only appear for racing and at one time spinnakers were banned, but now, after much controversy they are allowed. Few work boats have a spinnaker and they are usually borrowed from local yachtsmen.

The Truro River oyster boats, which is what the older generation call them, have developed within the traditions of South Cornwall. An open boat can be used in the Truro Fishery because they are working in sheltered waters, although when a southerly gale blows in over the ebb the boats are often working with their bowsprits slamming the wave tops. The present boats with the Terylene sails are worked harder than the wooden-hulled flax-sailed boats of the old days. All have Terylene sails now and some have two sets so that sail damage does not delay dredging. The man-made-fibre sails and ropes do not freeze hard like the old gear. The restrictive practices in the Truro Oyster Fishery have caused this work-boat type to continue developing right into the space age.

The 'old' *Six Brothers* racing. She
was built by Ferris at Restronguet,
probably in the 1880s

The Truro River-built *Beatrice* is
sailing back up to start another drift.
The faster the boat the more drifts
she can get in during the 9 am–3 pm
working time. She also has a small
working jib and a line for hauling the
staysail down, all to make boats
easier to sail while the oystermen
work the heavy dredges

The *Ivy* sails back up to start
another drift while the Looe-built
Caterina drifts down, 1974

TRAWLERS, LUGGERS AND OYSTER BOATS

The GRP hull *Three Sisters* looks
after herself while the men sort out
oysters in the moveable trays

Ron Laity's *Helen Mary* had only
been dredging a few days when seen
here in the autumn of 1974. It is
incredible that any genuine sailing
work boat should still be being built.
Apart from these, only a few sailing
trawlers and Thames barges have
been built since World War I

Tea break on Carrick Roads as the
Helen Mary sails back up wind. The
need for good inexpensive boats has
taken the work boats into man-made
materials. However, the nature of the
Truro River oyster fishery means
that there will probably always be a
living for a limited number of boats

The *George Glasson* racing under a cloud of sail she would never set for winter dredging

TRAWLERS, LUGGERS AND OYSTER BOATS

The summer races for oyster
dredgers provide a wonderful
spectacle. Overfishing has been
avoided by keeping the 'no power
boats' rule

Work boats *Serica, Victory,*
Magdalina, St Meloris and *Stella*
jockeying at the start of a race in 1968

8 Channel Traders

There was regular trade to
Teignmouth for china clay

The Finnish schooner *Gullkrona*, of
Mariehamn, leaving Weymouth 1939

The ports along the South Coast of England played a vital part in the development of small sailing ships until the mid-nineteenth century; then they drifted away to being more involved in the leisure industry. The reason was simple. This coast was obviously geographically well placed for trade with Europe and North America. That was until the Industrial Revolution, when new docking complexes at the major ports served by fast steamers made the simple rural ports only suitable for coastal trade.

The Devon ports of Salcombe and Dartmouth were deeply involved in the importation of fresh fruit. To the fruit schooners, speed was of the utmost importance, as they loaded fruit in the Eastern Mediterranean or West Indies and then literally raced to British ports before the fruit went bad. The trade was one of high risk but, if successful, high return. In Greece, where currants were loaded, it was even dangerous for masters and mates to go

ashore because they were liable to be captured by brigands and held for ransom. In the Azores, where much of the fruit came from, it was a well-organised trade, although dozens of schooners had to lie at anchor off Ponta Delgada and have their cargoes brought out by small boats. Once the last consignment was aboard the schooners recovered their anchors at once and clapped on all sails, which included stunsails, in an attempt to beat their rivals to Fresh Wharf in the Thames.

The topsail schooner, which later became almost universal in British small sailing ships, appears to have been greatly developed in the fruit trade because of its all-round performance. When the steamers started to take over the fast fruit cargoes, many of the schooners fell back into the coastal trade. This meant taking cargoes, mostly coal, into the shallow tidal ports, and the schooners with their deep, shapely hulls were totally unsuited for this kind

The Finnish schooner *Yxpila*, built 1920, discharging timber at Weymouth Harbour 1937. In the foreground is one of the Weymouth watermen's sailing boats, locally called a stuffy boat

of trade. However, the fruit schooners never lost their speed, even under a reduced sail-plan. It was the former fruit schooner *Uzziah* which in 1912 left Cuxhaven, Germany, loaded with salt and sailed the 722 miles to Plymouth in seventy-two hours. This meant that she averaged about ten knots, which was a deal faster than a small steamer of that time could have achieved.

The old sailing-ship men were overjoyed at such performances, but the trouble was that schooners could make record passages like this if they had favourable conditions. The final voyage of the brigantine *Undine* shows how even a powerful fast sailer could not overcome prolonged headwinds. She was built at Polruan, Fowey, to trade with pineapples from the West Indies, but in her old age became a Whitstable collier. Her last voyage started when she left Whitstable for the Tyne on 12 January 1917 and spent several miserable weeks banging about the

Italian brigantine drying sails at
East Quay, Poole, while being
loaded with Dorset clay from barges

Captain Horace Martell at the wheel of the Poole *Durlstone*

A coasting ketch, possibly *Antagonist*, beating out of Poole Harbour past Brownsea Island

The inshore fishing boats of
Southampton, The Solent and Poole
had a tall narrow gaff mainsail

North Sea, but just couldn't make any progress against the
everlasting northerly wind. Eventually the *Undine* ran
back to Gravesend for fresh stores, and then in a break in
the weather snatched a passage north only to be run down
by a steamer off Flamborough Head on 25 February.

During some of these winter voyages schooners just
vanished and no one ever knew what became of them.
This happened to the three-masted *Dairy Maid* of
Fleetwood which, like many traders, carried china clay
from Charlestown, Par and Teignmouth north to the
Mersey. The *Dairy Maid* was warped out of Charlestown's
tiny harbour in February 1915 and sailed out for Runcorn,
but no trace of her was ever seen again. One schooner
going missing was nothing when one realised that fifty
years previously whole fleets just vanished. One January

Trading ketches at Dell Quay at the
head of Chichester Harbour

night in 1866 seventy ships were counted anchored in Tor
Bay. They had come in to shelter, but in the night the gale
went round into south-south-east so that in the pitch black
a huge sea came roaring in. At dawn only eleven were still
at anchor; some had managed to beat off the lee shore, but
most had simply been overwhelmed.

The port of Weymouth was rather overshadowed by
the naval base of Portland Harbour. However, in the 1860s
Weymouth had 135 sailing ships most of which had been
built locally with timber brought from the New Forest.
The main occupation of these ships was bringing coal from
the Wear and Tyne to Weymouth and other South-
Country ports, but there was a regular trade with naval
stores from London. This ended after World War I, but
after this the Finnish schooners used to come every

summer to Weymouth with timber.

Although sailing ships departed in the nineteenth
century from the everyday events of the South-Country
ports, it is easy to overlook the fact that Poole sent ships in
the Newfoundland trade for nearly three hundred years.
In 1788 Poole was the leading port in this trade with twice
the tonnage of its rival Dartmouth. The Poole ships
crossed the Atlantic in the spring to fish cod off
Newfoundland. Later many families left the Poole area,
which has the most gentle climate in the British Isles, and
emigrated to the harsh environment of Newfoundland
because of the opportunities cod fishing created. By the
last stages of the Newfoundland trade all the fishing was
done by the settlers, and British home-country ships just
transported the salted cod to Europe.

Low tide at Rye. The two ketch
barges are the coasting type built at
Littlehampton and Rye

High tide at Rye. Moored next to the big boomie barge is one of the little double-ended lugsail barges which worked between Rye Harbour and the town

The Newfoundland trade was a particularly hard one, the bluff-bowed ships of the early nineteenth century had quite a battle just crossing the Atlantic, let alone living for months off the Newfoundland coast. In December 1833 the *Perseverance* returned to Poole leaking badly and her sails and rigging virtually in pieces. She had spent nearly a month at sea trying to make her way west. By this time the trade was in a decline and the Poole men were no longer willing to endure the hardships for the returns it brought. It shows just how awful it must have been if it was considered unbearable by the early Victorian working man. In 1834 there were still fifty-four Poole merchants operating in Newfoundland, but their counterparts back in Dorset had either gone bankrupt or put their ships in other trades.

Yet a century later Poole men were still going to sea in sail. In 1925 one seventeen-year-old seaman joined the two-masted topsail schooner *Sydney*, then one of the last sailers to trade from Guernsey. His wage was 15s (75p) a week when trading to the London River and £1 if the *Sydney* went north to Sunderland. Neither the young seaman nor the cook would go aloft to stow the square sails. This meant that the mate and skipper had to do all the work aloft, which of course was wrong, as the Master should have been at the wheel making the necessary decisions for the schooner's safety, not fighting heavy canvas fifty feet above the deck.

Often it was not the working conditions that made life on the schooners difficult, but the frustrations caused by hardy, resolute men being cramped up in a small area. It only needed poor food, lack of sleep and damp living-quarters to cause this underlying current to explode into violence. Probably the most happy ships were the ones with a crew from the smaller coastal ports where a rigid but self-imposed discipline helped to subdue the differences in temperament. Over their years at sea most men came to terms with the social problems; and indeed because their working lives—which then virtually meant their whole lives—were such a challenge, it gave them satisfaction. When men got on well in the same ship it created a special bond of human relationship. To say a man was a good shipmate was the highest compliment.

During the last years of sail the English Channel ports were abandoning schooners and adopting barges. The ketch barge *Alexandra* was built at Poole in 1891, and

Harveys of Littlehampton actually built some of the finest coasting barges. In the mid-Victorian period Harveys were building wooden ships for deep-water trades, but the steel ships of the Clyde and Wear superseded them. Harveys' last large vessel was the barque *Goodwood* which was launched in 1880 after having been on the stocks for three years while they tried to find a buyer. The yard now turned to coasting barges but, although this meant no great change in the way the yard was operated, it was a blow to John Harvey's pride. He always called the craft ketches and no one dared call them barges, at least not within his hearing. The yard built thirty-four superb ketch barges, but for the official yard photographs the tell-tale leeboards were removed so that the awful stigma of the word barge might not be associated with them.

Henry Hilder Harvey was the last member of the family running the yard until he retired after launching the *Wellholme* in 1916, but the yard continued to build *Wessex* in 1918 and finally *Moultonian* in 1919. Littlehampton and Rye had both flourished as shipbuilding centres because of the continual supply of good Sussex oak, but the Harvey family record was particularly good for, as well as undertaking repairs, they had regularly launched new ships over a period of seventy years. A great deal of their success was due to a good working relationship between the Harvey family and the skilled shipwrights. The departure of sail also coincided with a change in public attitudes: today large faceless organisations and trade unions have deliberately broken down trust between different sections of people in the same industry. The advantage of the small and completely independent commercial operation was that the problem could be solved on the spot without outside factions frustrating every decision.

The family unit was an important part of social order in the smaller ports, and the continual presence of successive generations gave the community a great sense of stability. Often the shareholders and crews of small sailing ships were all related. The Martells, who ended the long line of Poole sailing-ship owners, were just such a family. Captain Arthur Martell sailed his schooner *Regina* until she was requisitioned as a guardship in World War I. After the war she was refitted at Ashton & Kilners, Poole, and sailed by Alfred Martell until he died. She was then sold to Captain Harry Perches of Par, Cornwall.

A sailing vessel has to have
constant and skilful attention to
sails and rigging. At Rye the men are
working aloft on the smack *Lucy*

Captain Arthur Martell continued to sail the *Antagonist* as a family ship with his three sons. This ketch started off as a straight-stemmed, transom-sterned, tiller-steered craft but was gradually altered to being clipper-bowed, counter-sterned and wheel-steered. The *Antagonist* was a good all-round sailer; once, running free up the Firth of Forth with a cargo of grit from West Bay, Bridport, for Charlestown, she carried a squaresail right up under the Forth Bridge and kept pace with the coastal steamers. One of the great disadvantages of schooners and ketches was that they were very awkward to handle in confined waters. Often when bound up the Thames they would take a tug at Gravesend, but the *Antagonist* was once turned to windward right up to Greenwich. She had four headsails, and by the time she got there the crew's hands were raw after tending the sheets.

Captain Arthur Martell's sons were constantly on to him to put an engine in *Antagonist*, but he had spent a lifetime under sail and wouldn't hear of such a thing. The end of this family ship came tragically in 1922 when on passage from St Helens, Isle of Wight, to Newcastle, she was run down by a trawler fifteen miles off Flamborough Head. It was a perfectly clear day but the trawler simply didn't have anybody on lookout. She crashed through the port side of *Antagonist* and, as the ketch was loaded with railway metals, she sank in a matter of seconds. Horace and John, then just a boy of fourteen, were saved, but Captain Martell and Frederick were drowned.

In 1924 the Martells bought two more ships for the coasting trade. One was the steel ketch *Hanna*, built as the *Margaretha* of Waterhuizen in The Netherlands in 1915. Quite a number of steel sailing vessels were built in Germany and The Netherlands almost up to World War II. The *Hanna* loaded 160 tons and was sailed by Captain Arthur Martell Jr. Although a successful auxiliary trader she was sold to Captain Artie Watts of Exeter. After World War II she was the only South-Coast-owned sailer left trading and was eventually lost in the Channel Islands.

The other vessel the Martells bought was the Littlehampton-built *Durlstone*, a wooden ketch barge which loaded about 200 tons. For six-and-a-half years the *Durlstone* was in the Continental trade from southern England and mostly brought tiles from Antwerp and Brest. She was treated as an auxiliary sailer, with the engine running all the time at sea and her leeboards serving as fenders. This way she earned a living for her owners and crew. Actually it was her machinery which led to *Durlstone*'s loss. In February 1931 she was off the west coast of Jersey when the mate was in the engine room lighting the blowlamp which was used to start the winch motor needed to haul the mainsail. The skipper called down for the mate to give him a hand on deck. Probably while the crew were busy on deck the heavy rolling caused the methylated spirit bottle to get knocked over. Anyway, smoke was seen pouring out of the engine room and they were forced to abandon ship. Later they were picked up by the tanker *Linklight* and Captain Horace Martell's comment was 'We were lucky to get out of it'.

At Rye a man is clearing the silt away from the berths so that it is swept away on the ebb tide. This was done in some form at all tidal ports

9 Mostly Gaff and Spritsail

Sunset over London River barge roads

Colliers at Whitstable. When this
was taken in about 1902 there were
about thirty schooners and square-
riggers owned there by J.R. Daniels
and The Whitstable Shipping
Company

Twice a day the Atlantic Ocean comes flooding round the British Isles and into the North Sea. The northern half of the North Sea is exposed, but relatively deep, while at about South Shields the sea becomes progressively shallower. This means that two daily tides have less space to flow on both the flood and ebb runs. The shallow seabed makes the great volume of ever-moving tidal water race over the ground; then, just to add further confusion, there are numerous sandbanks on the Dutch, Belgian and East Anglian shores between which the tide boils through with the full weight of the Atlantic forcing it on.

Yet the tides are at least predictable while the weather is always changing; and when the wind freshens and meets this restless water moving in the opposite direction then the surface is cut up into short, steep, menacing seas.

The grey ever-shifting North Sea is a body of water

The brigantine *Undine* entering
Whitstable deeply loaded with coal

It was the difficult conditions of the North Sea which caused the gaff rig to be developed. The constant changes of wind force and direction meant that a highly versatile sail-plan was needed and the four-sided sail with a spar, the gaff, at the head, and much later a boom at the foot, proved to be highly effective. Until the beginning of the nineteenth century the Dutch and British were struggling for merchant supremacy and they developed the spritsail and gaff to suit their own conditions; but probably the political enmity forced different lines of development. For instance, the mussel-fishing hoogaars of Flushing were totally different to the Essex and Whitstable smacks, which did the same type of work on the other side of the North Sea. The Welsh oyster boats of Mumbles, however, on the other side of Britain, were almost indistinguishable from the nimble little Essex smacks.

The great trade of the North Sea was of course coal. Most East-Coast ports stood at the heads of shallow estuaries, often nothing more than a creek which dried out at low water. Sailing barges were adopted at most East-Coast ports in the 1880s, but Lowestoft and Whitstable both had coal delivered from the Tyne and Wear by small square-riggers right up to World War I. Whitstable stands on the open sea, so that barquentines and schooners could sail right up to the Pier Head. If they had been bound up an estuary they would have needed a tug, which is why the 'easier-to-maneuvre' sailing barges took the trade to estuary ports like Maldon and Colchester. At Whitstable the local owners banded together to form the Whitstable Shipping Company which ran a fleet of heavy and mostly rather elderly ships, not just in the coal trade, but also to Scandinavia and Russia after timber. Some of the Whitstable ships were real veterans, patched up and kept going as long as they could show a slight profit by undercutting the railways in hauling coal from the north.

The Canterbury coal merchant Fairbrass had the brig *Edward Fairbrass* built at Whitstable, and when the brigs went out of fashion she was taken ashore at Whitstable in 1875, cut in half and then lengthened to be relaunched as a new and larger barquentine, *Gratitude*. She went on to spend decades carrying coal for the London and Canterbury Gas Works. These were very much larger vessels than the barges which replaced them in most ports. The *Gratitude* loaded 350 tons, and another of the Whitstable Shipping Company's fleet, the barquentine

which nobody can ever grow to love, it is just too bad tempered. Perhaps it has influenced the people who have lived on its shores, for both the Dutch and the English have always been active and restless. In the age of sail this was the most congested area of water in the world. It was thick with fish until steam and then motor fishing vessels began their work. The North Sea was also the commercial highway in the centre of the great European community.

Strood Dock on the upper reaches of
the River Medway, 1905. The tiller-
steered barge *Gracey*, built 1867,
belonged to Goldsmiths

The barge *Gwynhelen* discharging ballast from Colne Point at Dagenham for the building of Ford's car factory, 1930

The steel coasting-barge *Will Everard* ashore at Bacton in 1936. The Cromer lifeboat is standing by, but the barge got off safely

The barge *Nellie Parker* in a stiff breeze off Mersea Island

Herbert, loaded 440 tons, while the spritsail barge *Will Everard*, one of the largest ever built, still only loaded about 250 tons. The *Will Everard* and *Cambria* were still bringing coal from Keadby under sail in the 1950s.

While researching this book I came across the hulk of an old Whitstable collier in Milford Haven. She had been the *Sela*, a brigantine built in 1859 and, like so many British coasters of the mid-Victorian period, was built on the other side of the Atlantic in Prince Edward Island. The *Sela* was registered at Faversham, like all the Whitstable colliers, and vessels of her size were regularly towed up this narrow Kent creek to discharge in that town. Under first Fairbrass and then the Whitstable Shipping Company the *Sela* had been pumped up and down the collier routes hundreds of times. As her hull showed signs of age, more skins of planking had been added until the *Sela's* sides were about 18in almost solid timber. She had gone to Neyland as a breakwater just after World War I when post-war freight markets slumped and it was impossible to find work for such an old carthorse of the coastal seas.

The only sailing coastal trading vessels to survive the shipping slump of the early 1920s in any numbers were the Thames spritsail barges. The spritsail rig crops up in some form in most underdeveloped countries and it was once widely used throughout Northern Europe. In the nineteenth century there was a big swing to using the gaff rig in some form; only in the Thames Estuary was the spritsail really developed to provide a labour-saving form of coastal transport. The early spritsail barges worked just in the Port of London, but proved so effective that by the 1890s spritsail barges capable of making passages to the Continent were being built in large numbers throughout south-eastern England.

By the liberal use of winches and an ingenious layout of running rigging the large sail area of the barges could be controlled by two men. The smaller 60-ton barges just did river work, usually between the Thames and Medway and within the London dockland. Then there were the 150-ton barges trading between the London docks and smaller ports on the east and south coasts. Lastly, there were the real coasters which took anything anywhere. Before World War I they quite happily loaded a freight for Germany or Ireland, but in the 1920s they were driven out of the Continental ports by the state-subsidised coasters from The Netherlands. The river work was taken on by lorries, so this left only the trade of moving imported raw materials from the London Docks to the country ports.

Sailing barges found a slot in the freight market working to places like Whitstable, Faversham, Colchester, Mistley and Ipswich. All these were just far enough away from the London dock system to make land transport too expensive on lorries which only loaded 7–10 ton and went over archaic road systems. After World War II the railways became state owned and quickly lost their urge to move bulk goods competitively, so for quite a long period barges could just hold their own. At the same time, taking grain from London to the country mills did not quite bring in enough returns to warrant building new modern coasters, although each year saw more barges fitted with engines.

Barges also went on trading under sail long after other similar traders had gone because many people wanted them to. They represented the very last of the glorious age of British Sail and that drew men to them. In 1955 I sailed on the auxiliary mulie *Will Everard* and a year later as mate on the Mistley sailing barge *Xylonite*, and I experienced and took part in the wonderful sense of comradeship that those final years created. Some of the older skippers had stayed with sail because they knew no other way to get a living, but most skippers were in their early twenties and mates were teenagers. Everyone knew that the unique situation of genuine working sail could not last much longer and were willing to try to make it last. However, at this time, there was a strong feeling that barges should be finished with when the last cargo had been delivered under sail.

In November 1956 the *Xylonite* loaded sunflower seed for Mistley from a ship in the Lower Pool of London. Since it was blowing hard from the north-east we sailed down to Sheerness to wait for better weather to make a passage to Harwich. The weather didn't improve and over the next week all the remaining sailing barges, plus the auxiliary barges, came down from the London River to join us windbound. Then one raw grey December dawn we all made sail together and headed up the Swin Channel. There was the *Anglia, Marjorie, May, Memory, Portlight, Spinaway C, Venture* and of course *Xylonite*—all the barges left genuinely working except *Cambria*, which was said to be lying in the Thames waiting for a freight. By dusk the deeply loaded barges crept into Harwich with

Harold Robertson on the *Redoubtable*. Skipper Robertson had the reputation for making fast passages in the *Redoubtable*. In the 1930s, when this barge was fitted with a huge sail area for racing, she once blew out eleven topsails in twelve months. The owners did not mind this type of damage because it showed the skipper was having a go and not lying windbound. *Redoubtable* is very beamy because she was intended to load bulky cargoes for the Mistley cattle food mills. Bargemen said that so long as she stood up the barge had to go forward. She usually had a two-man crew and could take 180 tons on the London to Yarmouth run. Once she delivered 200 tons of barley from London to Mistley and even loaded 220 tons on river lighterage work. Having a low rail and little sheer she caught little windage, and she could be turned up a narrow creek

Barge sails are left white for the
first year to wash oils out of the
flax. The black spot on the topsail of
Spinaway C shows that she
belonged to Cranfields of Ipswich,
1963

Sailing barges waiting to discharge
at Pauls, Ipswich, in 1910. These
mills provided work which was to
be the last undertaken by sailing
cargo vessels in Britain

a dying breeze. It was the last time so many barges sailed
in company as the two steel barges *Portlight* and *Xylonite*
dropped out of trade later that winter.

The *Memory* was found spasmodic work until 1960,
although the last regular trade for sailing barges was
bringing grain from London to the Ipswich mills. But
again in 1960 the Ipswich mill-owners, Pauls, decided to
finally sell *Marjorie* and *Anglia.* These were their last two
sailing barges, but they still had wooden ex-sailing barges
working under power. When they finished in 1974 one of
them, the *Ena*, was rerigged for the firm's employees to

sail. The other Ipswich fleet-owners, Cranfield Bros, kept
the *Venture* until 1963, sold the *May* the following year and
after this just used the *Spinaway C* for lightering and racing
until selling her in 1967. Her departure from Ipswich
marked the end of the last fleet of pure sailing cargo vessels
in Northern Europe. Only the *Cambria*, which was owned
at Pin Mill just down river from Ipswich, sailed her lonely
way until 1970, picking up what few freights were still
available. Even after this the *May*, now owned in the
London River and fitted with an engine, carried a few
small freights.

The barges *Lord Roberts* and *May* passing under Tower Bridge on a promotion charter in 1971. Even though barges no longer carry cargoes most still have to pay their way by chartering

The tug *Imperial* towing a brig out of
Lowestoft

Cranfield's auxiliary barge *Orinoco*
leaving Ipswich for London in
January 1954

The Broadland wherry *Cornucopia* of
Stalham

The huge gaff sails of the wherries allowed them to sail close to the bank in the shallow rivers of the East Anglian Broads

The Wherrymen used to hack down any tree that might grow to stop their all-important wind. With the departure of the wherries the trees grew up

10 Smacks, Beach Boats and Cobles

The North Norfolk crab boats were
evolved to suit beaching on a long
shallow shore

Leigh men unloading shellfish in sacks from a bawley. Leigh and Southend bawleys also worked in the Sea Reach for shrimps

Inshore fishing boats were an intricate part of every local environment. The fishermen of the Thames used a double-ended open boat called a Peter boat, but these died out when the river became badly polluted. The Medway fishermen went on using identical craft which they called dobles. The Medway still survives even now as one of the old 'free' fisheries. In fact it is not free at all: it is only men who have served an apprenticeship who can fish in the twenty miles of tidal estuary above Sheerness. Most of the freemen in Victorian times lived in Strood and kept their boats in Pelican Creek. From here it was about thirteen miles down to the open sea and the men often rowed this distance. Coming back in, if the wind dropped and the tide was against them, they put the dobles ashore and walked home carrying their shrimps—which had to be

The Whitstable oyster dredger *Victory*. Variations of this counter-sterned, cutter-smack type were used all along the East Coast

quickly boiled in the coppers at the back of each cottage.

In the 1890s the Strood fishermen began buying bawleys. These were decked craft of about 35-40ft long and carried a very lofty sail plan. Len Wadhams, Chamberlain of The Rochester Oyster and Floating Fishery, told me how when his father and uncles went round to Milton Creek and bought the bawley *Minion* in 1903 they were tremendously proud to be the owners of such a craft after working the little open dobles. Just before World War I there were eighteen sailing bawleys

at Strood and more just down river at Chatham and Gillingham. A few dobles went on smelt fishing above Rochester Bridge while the bawleys went trawling and earned their owners money dredging oysters off Cockham Woods.

Then industry and pollution came to the Medway and the fishery trailed off, but the fishermen kept their bawleys and were very reluctant to part with them. Some bawleys just fell to pieces with old age but very few were sold. A few survived, were motorised and are still at Strood Pier:

Southwold fishermen with drift net in 1904

the *Iverna*, built across the Medway at Gill's Rochester yard in 1893; the *Hilda Marjorie*, built at Harwich in about 1900; and the *Minion*, which once was part of the fleet which worked from Sittingbourne's Crown Quay before pollution drove them out of this creek very early in this century.

All the fishermen who started in sail that I have spoken to hotly deny that the word bawley is derived from 'boiler boat'. However the main feature of the bawley was its very wide beam which gave stability so that the water was not spilt from the coppers as they sailed back boiling their shrimps. When sail was used on the East Coast, the Essex fishermen used to gather at Harwich during the shrimping season. Every night between sixty and a hundred craft came racing back into the harbour to get their catch on to the night train. What a sight they must have been, the bawleys from Leigh and Harwich, sitting like ducks on the water under their vast spread of canvas, and in among them the powerful cutter smacks from Tollesbury. If there was no wind then craft were rowed in on the tide. The

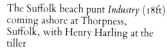

The Suffolk beach punt *Industry* (18ft) coming ashore at Thorpness, Suffolk, with Henry Harling at the tiller

Harwich bawleys did not have any regular moorings, they just let their anchors go for the night in whatever part of the estuary was sheltered. Sometimes this meant rowing their heavy foot or hack boats home over a mile against wind and tide. Next morning, often before daylight, they were off again heaving in fathoms of heavy chain over the hand-spike windlass. Then, under the heavy canvas sails, they ghosted out to sea in the grey, raw half-light of dawn.

The smacks of Whitstable, Essex and The Wash were all rather similar, but although there was undoubtedly some exchange of boats and ideas, all these types developed independently at the same time. Virtually all these inshore smacks were gaff cutters and, because they spent their working lives in narrow channels, they had masts stepped well forward to make them reliable for going to windward. The Wash ports of King's Lynn, Wisbech, Sutton Bridge, Fosdyke and Boston were all well inland up long and narrow rivers and it often took the smacks a whole day just to work out into The Wash. The tide on the flood runs at five knots, and when the wind was against the tide out in the open deeps it quickly built up an incredibly short steep sea. To be in a gale in the Lynn Deeps in a sailing shrimper may not sound as dramatic as rounding Cape Horn but it was really just as dangerous. The loss of life in The Wash was high for an inshore fishery.

When cockling, the fishermen had to run ashore on the isolated sandbanks and gather the shellfish at low water. This was a great worry when the weather was bad as they could be caught on a lee shore. The Lynn smack *Mystery* and her crew of four were lost this way. The smack was broken up by the breakers before she had enough water to sail clear. The Norfolk yoll *Edward VII* once had to be left in the same way but she was salvaged two days later. Yet to earn a living the fishermen were forced to take chances. The Boston *Freda & Norah*, which Worfolk built in 1912 as the *George & Charles*, once spent a whole week in The Wash without getting anything. Finally they got amongst the sprats and kept on taking fish until the deck was almost level with the water. They got back safely with the whole 20 tons and sold their catch for £3 per ton.

The cost of building The Wash boats seems incredible now. The Boston *Alice* cost £80 new, the Norfolk yoll *Baden Powell* cost £50 when Worfolk built her in 1902, while the smack *Telegraph* was £120 four years later. The Edwardian era saw most of the coastal, sailing, fishing craft reaching a peak in design and number. In The Wash, Lynn had the most, with well over a hundred boats; there was not room for them all in Fisher Fleet so the larger boats had to lie in the Dock.

The 58ft *Britannia*, built in 1915, was the last sailing smack built. Worfolks went on to build the slightly larger *Grace & Ellen* the following year but she was fitted with an auxiliary. Before the Worfolks came to Lynn most of the new boats came from Yarmouth, while the Boston smack-builders were the Gostelows. The *Britannia* was a whelker.

These anchored, often a week at a time, out on the whelk grounds near the Dudgeon Lightvessel. An 18ft open boat which was towed astern was used to lay the whelk pots. Since they were working in the open North Sea it was quite common for the boat to get separated from the smack and to have to make for the land. Whelk boats were rowed into Yarmouth on at least two occasions.

For one day a year the fishermen forgot the troubles of their occupation and had a race. The first Boston regatta was in 1849 when it seems that as well as smacks with their high-peaked mainsails there were several small open boats rigged as schooners, with spritsail and jibs, taking part. This race seems to have faded out and the smacks are now remembered as racing off the seaside towns of Skegness and Hunstanton. The *Telegraph* won Skegness Regatta in 1908 and her crew were delighted with the £5 prize money. They spent a happy week drinking and singing round the pubs while the owner William Stringer waited, not very patiently, back at Boston for his smack to return.

At Lynn their race was taken very seriously and most of the fleet took a week off to get ready for it. The start was off Fisher Fleet at about 6 am to give the fleet time to sail the twenty-one-mile course and finish later in the afternoon. The smacks, which in The Wash usually meant decked cutters with topmasts, made one class. The next class was the smaller pole-masted cutters with the long open hatch for working in. These were usually known as trawlers or shrimpers and were fitted with coppers and hand-operated capstans. Lastly, there were the Norfolk yolls, double-ended and often clinker built, but still cutters, which usually went cockling.

Looking back, the fishermen reckon that they did more damage to their boats in a day's racing than in a year's work. All this passed with the coming of engines in the 1920s and Frank Castleton remembers how keen the Lynn men were to do away with the uncertainties of sail. He was taking a smack away at nineteen years old when his father was ill and later worked the 50ft *Firefly* LN 10. The owner was a lady who played the violin. When he went to settle the accounts with her she was glad of an audience and insisted on playing to him. Frank Castleton owned the *Queen Alexandra* afterwards, which was reputed to have been a noted racer. The Lynn men abandoned sail early for safety reasons but kept and used sails right into the 1950s for the same reason.

The small open Suffolk beach boat is totally different from the fifie from the Firth of Forth, yet both are leaving Lowestoft in search of herring

In 1975 there were still a few of the old sailing smacks active in the Lynn fleet and kept in the traditional Fisher Fleet, including the yoll *Baden Powell*. Incredibly, her builder's sons, Gerald and Bill Worfolk, then both in their eighties, were still at work building a new wooden motor ketch to cross the Atlantic. The Worfolk brothers believe they have built about 650 boats. As well as the workmanship, it was the material that went into these sailing smacks that allowed them to survive seventy years of hard work. The *Rose of Old England* was about this age when wrecked in The Wash. Her mast was black and chafed, but under this the pitch pine was found to be in perfect order. The *Lily May* was the last Lynn shrimp trawler to work under sail only, because her owner would not accept an engine. The *Lily May* was later sold to join the Cornish oyster fleet, but although fast, she was not as handy as the smaller Truro River boats for dredging in the Carrick Roads and she became a yacht.

A Moray Firth zulu and Firth of Forth
fifies rowing out of Lowestoft. The
Scottish drifters came south for the
East Anglian herring fishery every
autumn

The Ramsgate trawler has just enough wind to get out of Lowestoft without paying for a tug

The Lowestoft trawler *Annie Ethel*, built by R. Jackman at Brixham in 1908, has her bowsprit run in while she is inside the harbour pierheads

Lowestoft trawlers being towed to sea

Traditional craft were of course evolved to suit just one set of conditions but there was a tremendous difference in the actual performance of individual craft. The smacks from the same yards were different; even the ones which were supposed to have been sister ships were not the same under sail. Aldous of Brightlingsea built most of the Essex smacks, and not one is truely the same as any other because every fisherman had his own idea of the perfect working boat. The Essex smacks were very much influenced by the prevailing yacht design, although the beautiful counter-sterns were popular because it gave more working deck space. There were very roughly two types of Essex smacks: the smaller ones stayed in the estuary while the large powerful cutters, mostly from Brightlingsea and Tollesbury, worked around the coasts. Most of the fishing villages had more smacks than could hope to earn a living in the home waters. This forced the Victorian Essex smackmen to be little short of pirates when it came to oysters. They usually kept together so as they could meet local opposition in force. Even now there are men in Cornwall who can recall the fear and hate that the sight of those powerful smacks caused when they were seen beating in from the sea past Falmouth.

To the Colne and Blackwater men nothing was sacred and they would raid other East Coast rivers, although God help the man who was caught with a dredge down in any of their beds. In time these smacks worked out most of the natural oyster beds, the Maldon smacks are alleged to have finished off the Hamford Water oysters while the Suffolk rivers of Deben and Ore were worked by the Stokers of West Mersea. Indeed in the Deben, my own home river, it is remembered that Mersea smacks arrived in the 1920s and stayed until they had virtually got the last oyster.

By World War II oystering had become a peaceful occupation and most of the big smacks were left to rot on the saltings. After that war the *Our Boys* was still working under sail from West Mersea. In 1953 I remember meeting the Maldon *Polly* with trawl down in the Blackwater. With her patched sails and two very veteran smackmen she certainly looked like the last of her breed, which is what she was. Now about forty Essex smacks are still sailed for pleasure. They are smarter and have lost some of the mystique which goes with genuine working boats, but they are a link with the region's maritime traditions.

With beach boats, the sailing versions did not outlive

their working lives, but modern boats are still built on the traditional lines, such as the beach boats that Frank Knights of Woodbridge has built for the Aldeburgh fishermen. The crabbers of North Norfolk are still the traditional types, while inshore fishermen between the Humber and Berwick have kept the coble.

Most fishermen would prefer larger and faster craft, but they have kept to the traditional hull shapes because they alone are best for the local conditions. The East Anglian beach boats and the cobles are sometimes built a little larger today because they never have to be rowed and are hauled up the beach mechanically. Of course the number of boats has been steadily reduced as the North Sea fish stocks have been worked out.

Beam trawl being hauled aboard William Stringer's Boston smack *Freda & Norah*, 1927

From the shelter of Fisher Fleet the Lynn smacks sailed out into the labyrinth of The Wash channels. Of all the smacks that Worfolk built, those still working after seventy years, under power, were *Gladys, Shamrock, Susannah, Queen Alexandra, King Edward VII, Baden Powell* and the ex pilot cutter *Eric Brown*

The Boston smack *Olive*. Often to get down the five-mile Haven to The Wash smacks had to be rowed or towed from the bank by the crew

The Mussel Stage, Skirbeck
Quarter, Boston, with the *Annie* and
other boats, 1928. Forty-seven years
later the motorised smacks *Freda &*
Norah, Retreiver II, Majestic, Pam
ex *Bertha* and *Esther* were still
amongst the largest craft working
the prolific Wash prawn, shrimp,
mussel and cockle fishery from
Boston. The *Britannia* was sold
after sinking—the result of getting
ashore in fog in The Haven in 1968

The Boston cockle boat *Alice* BN1.
Like the shrimpers she has a flat
counter-stern, while some of the big
Wash smacks, particularly those
built by Worfolk, had round counter-
sterns

The Bridlington coble *Doris*
taking summer trippers, 1908

11 Humber Keels, Billyboys and Sloops

A wooden keel with reefed mainsail in Stainforth and Keadby canal at Thorne

The steel Humber sloop *Phyllis* entering the Humber Dock, Hull, in 1937

numbers with the coming of the Industrial Revolution. They provided a cheap form of transport which was of course vital in any successful and profitable form of industry.

The keels never went to sea, in fact they were sometimes a problem to sail even in the Humber. They always worked the tide and usually only sailed when it was in their favour. For coastal work the Humber ports had their billyboys, which were a kind of sea-going keel. Originally these were cutter-rigged like the *Sulpho*. She, and other single-masted billyboys owned by Anderson of Howden Dyke, traded with fertiliser between the Humber and The Wash. Billyboys which went farther afield were schooners and later ketches, and they had high rails to keep the sea off the decks. In 1900 there were twenty-five coasting billyboys owned at Barton Haven. Barton seamen called the mizzen-mast a dickie and consequently a ketch became known to them as a dickie.

The last billyboy in the Humber-Thames trade was the *Brilliant Star*, but the last Barton billyboy finished in 1924 when the *New Eagle* was wrecked on Barton Ness and the *Evelyn* was broken up. Nine years later the old *Liberty* was broken up; she had a rig which under today's terms is a gaff cutter, but the men who sailed her would have classed her as a sloop billyboy. Quite a number of billyboys were owned in The Wash ports, particularly King's Lynn.

The craft on the south bank of the Humber were mostly engaged in running building materials across to Hull. The Humber has a fast-flowing tide-stream and as, lower down, it is open to the North Sea, this was no place for a keel. So owners here began putting a gaff mainsail on to keel hull types, and these were called Humber sloops. Most of the sloops were built of steel and had one long hatch. In the summer they sometimes made short coastal passages. The larger sloops like the *Phyllis, John William* and the *Lilian May*, were about 65ft long and could load from 110 to 130 tons, by which time the water was level with the deck amidships. The sloops which traded up the Market Weighton Canal had to have a reduced beam of 14ft 10in to get through the Weighton Lock. This made them faster, particularly the *Ousefleet*. Of course all the sloops, like the keels and billyboys, had leeboards to help them to grip the water when beating against the wind.

Even though the keels and sloops never really went to sea it was difficult enough for them in bad weather on the

Like most other estuaries the Humber had its own type of barge for purely local transport. These were called keels and were propelled amazingly successfully by a simple square sail. Leading from the Humber are hundreds of miles of navigable rivers and waterways, so that a wide area of central England could be served by the keels. Like the Thames barges the Humber keels increased greatly in

The sloop billyboy *Sulpho* at Stockwith on the River Trent in 1906. On the deck are Captain William Wheldrake and his wife and son

Humber estuary. The *Annie Maud*, a wooden keel built at Thorne in 1893, once got ashore on the Pudding Pie Sand in the open Humber during a gale and was sunk, but eventually, after several attempts, she was successfully salvaged a few months later. The sloop *Burgate* was beating up from Hull on the last of the flood tide when the skipper misjudged the entrance of Barton Haven, and as he couldn't get in he was obliged to anchor. While he was waiting for the next flood tide the wind increased to gale force, and with the ebb the *Burgate* dragged six miles down the open estuary. All that could be seen from the shore was the mast in breaking water and everyone thought that she would be overwhelmed, but the next day the *Burgate* returned safely to Barton.

Throughout January and February 1924 the sloop *John & Annie* of South Ferriby managed to break two booms even though her mainsail had been reefed. The keels were often delayed in the winter when the waterways were frozen over. However, they were amazingly good at sailing in the narrow waterways. Their way of sailing under a bridge was to drop the square sail to the deck so that the sail hung down 'athwart' either side of the hull. Then the mast was lowered, but the sail hanging over the sides kept the keel moving. Down on the open Humber estuary they sometimes had to wear the keels round when beating to windward. The Lincolnshire (ie, now Humberside south bank) sloops, on the other hand, went about more easily.

The Knottingley keel *William* traded regularly with coal

The keel *Annie Maud* at anchor some
time between 1929 and 1932 when
Fred Schofield was her master

The skipper and his wife helping the keel *Danum* through a 'shy rack'

The steel sloop *Valiant* loading chalk for bank repairs at Sprotborough on the River Don. Captain Jim Barley is standing on the foredeck

The *Broomfleet* racing in Barton
Sloop Regatta with the crew
squatting on the cabin deck to reduce
wind resistance

down to Hedon Haven, but most keels regarded Hull as
their limit for their trading. Most keels brought coal down
to Hull and then the skipper tried to fix a freight back
inland. This could be delivering artificial fertiliser to a
farmer on a canal-side bank, or timber to a merchant in a
small town, or the raw materials for factories in the
midlands. Keels were built to fit the locks on different

waterways, so there were the Sheffield-size keels, Barnsley-
size and Driffield-size all of which, as they traded right
inland, were slightly smaller.

Because keels were scattered over such a wide area it is
difficult to assess their numbers, but even in the 1930s there
were believed to be about 2,000 working wholly or partly
under sail. In 1935 150 keels were once counted delivering

The last Barton Sloop Regatta was
sailed in 1929

coal to trawlers at Hull, and J. Barraclough & Co alone
had fifteen sloops trading then. All these vanished abruptly
with World War II. I remember going up Old Harbour,
Hull, in 1955 on the *Will Everard* and it was packed with
keels drifting on the tide. At night they proved something
of a problem as we had difficulty in spotting them in the
dark, but none had even a mast by that time.

Although the Humber and its tributaries are the longest
connecting inland waterways in the British Isles, its fast-
flowing tides and industrial landscape have in the past
made it overlooked as a pleasure-boating area, so it was
really not until the mid-1970s that we were able to see a
successful attempt to restore a Humber keel for sailing.
The Humber Keel and Sloop Preservation Society has
bought the steel keel *Comrade*; she had been working as a
motor barge but the Society intends getting her back
under sail. At York another group is restoring the wooden
keel *Annie Maud* as a museum ship.

The sloop *Yokefleet* was owned by
H. Williamson & Co, brickmakers
at Broomfleet on the Market Weighton
Canal

12 The Sail Revival

The replica square-rigged ketch *Nonsuch* was built to celebrate The Hudson's Bay Company's 300th Anniversary. This replica was a problem to sail and was shipped out to Canada

It was the upheaval of World War I and the lengthy world trade recession which followed in its wake that finally marked the end of the sailing-ship era. Of course most people realised long before this great and bloody European struggle for world power that technical progress was bound to make sail obsolete. British owners almost totally abandoned deep-water sailing ships before World War I. In the 1880s and early 1890s almost every major port in the world would have been packed with huge square-riggers flying the Red Ensign, yet barely thirty years later only a handful of them remained. The glorious era of sail reached its peak and was gone in a very short space of time.

On the coast, trading vessels and fishing boats lasted longer than the lofty deepwatermen, but the story was the same. In 1900 sail was still the normal form of transport, but by the early 1930s it was reduced to little groups of elderly craft eking out a modest living by picking up freights which the steamers and Dutch motor coasters couldn't be bothered with. At first men could hardly believe that after centuries of usefulness, sailing ships could really have vanished, but they had. Then began the great race to record as much as possible about them. Strangely it was quite a long time before people began to try to preserve the actual ships. The first and perhaps the most impressive was the restoration of HMS *Victory*, which was finished in 1928 after six years' work.

In most cases it was just not practical to preserve every former working craft; usually it is left until only a few of a particular type remain and then there is a desperate scramble to save just one.

A traditional craft can be defined as a type which was evolved by trial and error in one location and usually built of local materials. The design was altered to suit the prevailing fashions of each generation. The revival of traditional sail is a deliberate attempt to restore working boats, not just as museum pieces, but to find some reason for keeping them actually sailing. Usually this is done by dedicated individuals working in isolation to achieve their particular form of nostalgia. This movement seems to have developed independently in most western nations with a strong maritime past. In Britain the two main areas where the traditional sail revival is most active are the West Country and the Thames Estuary.

The most extreme form of this interest in the past is to

Like many other wood carvings for restored sailing ships the figure-head of the *Falls of Clyde* was carved by Jack Whitehead of the Isle of Wight

actually recreate historical legends by building replicas of famous ships. In spite of very little being known about the original ship, a 260 gross-ton replica of the seventeenth-century *Mayflower* was built at Brixham in 1956. J. Hinks & Son of Appledore, north Devon, have become well known for building replicas, notably the *Nonsuch* in 1968 and the *Golden Hinde* in 1973. Building a true replica is a complex operation and there is always the temptation to slip into using more recent methods and construction materials than were used for the original vessel. Between 1892 and 1975 there appear to have been only twenty-two vessels constructed in the whole world which can be counted as being serious replicas and only about eight of these have been sailed extensively, so that there is still a great deal more to be discovered by the use of replicas.

Whenever possible it is best to restore an existing vessel to its original state. With the huge deepwatermen, they are often restored far from their place of origin in whatever part of the world fate left them. The four-masted full-rigged ship *Falls of Clyde* was built by Russell & Company in 1878 for the Glasgow Falls Line, but she has been restored in Honolulu. The much smaller iron barque *James Craig* is being restored in Australia because she was once a unit of J.J. Craig's fleet, but she was built at Sunderland in 1874 as the *Clan MacLeod* for Thomas Dunlop's Clan Line. In the case of these large vessels it is virtually impossible to get them back into a state where they could go to sea again. However with small commercial craft it is possible to get them back to sailing order. The greatest successes have been with the spritsail barges in the Thames Estuary. In 1967 I counted thirty barges capable of making a passage under sail, but by 1975 this number had risen to some forty-five barges.

Although most East Coast creeks and anchorages have a band of traditional boat-owners the little Essex estuary port of Maldon is the centre of the traditional craft movement. From about 1960 Maldon has been a heartening place to visit because a continual stream of traditional craft have been given a new lease of life here.

Across the North Sea in The Netherlands they have adapted the traditional boat lines to create a whole new generation of yachts, but on East Anglian and Kent coasts many individuals have striven hard to restore old work boats. There is a healthy dislike of synthetic materials and preference for wooden craft with canvas or flax sails.

The replica *Golden Hinde* is seen here entering San Francisco after taking six months to sail from Britain. Adrian Small was master of both *Nonsuch* and *Golden Hinde*. Sailing a replica means virtually adopting the same attitudes and having the same knowledge as the men who sailed the originals

The only large square-riggers now
seen in British ports are the training
ships of other nations. Here are the
Russian four-masted barque
Kruzenstern and the Polish *Dar
Pomorza* about to leave Portsmouth,
1974

The 1974 Tall Ships Race was like
the lifting of a curtain, because here at
last on show in the western
democratic countries of Europe were
the Russian sail training-ships. At
Portsmouth are *Kruzenstern, Dar
Pomorza* and the Russian
Tovarisch. The *Dar Pomorza* had won
the square-rigger class two years
before and this seems to have
encouraged the Russians. The
Tovarisch won the 1974 Copenhagen
Gdynia Race

The training-ships came to Britain in 1974 to take part in the Parade of Sail in the Solent. Here the *Kruzenstern* takes the salute from Prince Philip on the Royal yacht *Britannia* off Cowes

Crew of the *Charlotte Rhodes*,
Charlie Marsden, Mitch Mitchell,
Pete Lucas, mate, John MacKinnon,
Captain A.B.J. Macreth. From the
charterers, Philips Electrologica,
Peter Hancock and Herbert Beven

Charlotte Rhodes in the Irish Sea

A sizeable fleet of traditional craft has reappeared, each one representing countless hours of hard work and devotion. The races for barges, smacks and traditional gaff craft have provided tremendous incentive for craft restoration. Although they are sailed as a leisure activity, most of them are not yachts; they are the indigenous craft of the area deliberately preserved, not as museum pieces, but as the continuation of a local maritime culture.

It was really the higher wages and shorter working time which became general in the 1950s that allowed people more time to devote to interests like restoring old boats. Although this revival came in time to save Thames barges, unfortunately most of the British trading schooners and ketches had already gone. In 1959 I sailed in the Baltic, and every island still had schooners and galeases while The Sound between Denmark and Sweden was alive with them. At Copenhagen there was even a four-masted schooner discharging, but, like the rest, she appeared to be operating as a power vessel. A few years later the building of more road bridges and the introduction of faster modern craft quite suddenly rendered the vast fleet of Baltic traders obsolete and they came on the market very cheaply.

Many of these Baltic traders had short careers as yachts,

Three-masted topsail schooner
Charlotte Rhodes of BBC TV
Onedin Line

Jilly Cooper of the *Sunday Times* and
the author on *Charlotte Rhodes* in
Loch Ness

The *Esther Lohse* was built in Denmark during World War II when fuel was short. Off Brightlingsea she is passing the *Will Everard*, a barge which has also been rerigged

but some have been subjected to worthwhile projects in order to get them back under sail. Most of these traders had been built more recently than their British counterparts. The *New Endeavour*, which was rerigged at Ramsgate, began as the *Dana* when built by Ring Andersen at Svendborg, Denmark, in 1919. The wooden *Eolus*, which was later fitted out as a barquentine at Ramsgate, had actually been built as late as 1948 in Sweden. The *Eolus* proved too large to finance and became a white elephant, although after a few years of lying at Ramsgate and Portsmouth she finally made a world voyage which ended abruptly at Singapore.

Many Baltic traders came to grief simply because their owners failed to find a way to make them pay their keep. The galease *Solvig* was just large enough to carry the maximum of twelve passengers, but not so large that her upkeep costs exceeded her earnings in the East Coast charter work. Some of the barge and Baltic trader-owners in the Thames Estuary have been able to create regular work to finance their craft. The Davis brothers at Brightlingsea started with the little galease *Clausens Minde*, sold her, and returned to the Baltic and bought the slightly larger *Nora Av Ven*. After this they bought the three-masted schooner *Esther Lohse* which they virtually rebuilt before resuming their charter work. The three-masted *Golden Cachalot* also proved successful in passenger work after being refitted near Faversham, although she went to Central America. The three-masted *Jylland* was rigged near Maldon and then she departed for the West Indies.

The Danish trader *Meta Jan* might have done the same, but after being rerigged as the *Charlotte Rhodes* at Dartmouth she won instant fame through appearing in a

The brigantine *Marques* sailing out
from her base at Charlestown,
Cornwall

The galease *Solvig* became a yacht
and was lost in 1974 when she
dragged anchor at Ibiza

television series. After this she has been able to pay her
way by publicity cruises. The *Charlotte Rhodes* sail-plan is
based more or less on that of the *Result* and the *Rhoda
Mary*. The Danes had suggested her short topmast because
they were thinking of her as just a sail-using power vessel.
Under her present sail-plan *Charlotte Rhodes* tends to carry
a lot of weather helm, and this was corrected by putting a
reef in the mainsail.

Although she, like many other Baltic traders, had begun
in deep water, there is no doubt that these boats had lasted
longer because they had worked in tideless waters. They
were not subjected to the tremendous hull strains that the
British schooners had when taking the ground while
loading. By the mid 1970s the Baltic was no longer a
source of cheap former sailing traders; but a few still came,
like the smart Exeter-based *IP Thorsoe*, the steel *Eye of the
Wind* ex *Merry*, and the Leith-based wooden schooner
Christian Bach which was built as a motor ketch in 1953.
Instead, some—like the *Marques* and the *Pascual
Flores*—came from the Spanish Mediterranean. The British
barquentine *Regina Maris* had been a Baltic trader
converted by two Norwegian brothers who made some
spectacular world voyages in her.

These are real sailing ships and each has its own strong
character, but in spite of their age and beauty the sea does
not treat them with any particular respect. The wind
blows just as hard now as it did a hundred years ago. Of
course every sailing-ship passage has its difficulties, but
traditional ships must be in a state to withstand the
ultimate challenge that the sea will inevitably present.

The 44ft Brightlingsea smack *ADC*
and barge *Mirosa* coming up to win
their classes in the 1974 Colne Race.
Both of these have been completely
rerigged with proper traditional sails

The 36ft *Gracie* and 39ft *Iris* at the start of the West Mersea Smack Race, 1971. So many boats have been restored on the East Coast that former barge skipper Jim Lawrence has started up as a traditional sail-maker at Brightlingsea

The 40ft Whitstable smack *Stormy Petrel*, like the East Coast traditional craft, is still sailed without an engine

The 38ft Essex smack *Peace*, built in
1909, was one of the last of this
type built

The 47ft Whitstable smack *Rosa & Ada* has been completely restored by Tony Winter. He had previously rerigged the barge *Lord Roberts* with gear salvaged from about twenty barges that had been unrigged

Barges setting their gear before the Pin Mill Race, 1972

The 15ft *Prudence*, a wooden clinker
boat built by W. Cook & Son,
Maldon, 1973, on the lines of the
Essex fisherman's winkle brig

The *Kitty* has been rerigged and very
ably sailed by her skipper owner
John Fairbrother, so that as a charter
barge she has continued to earn a
living under sail only

Map

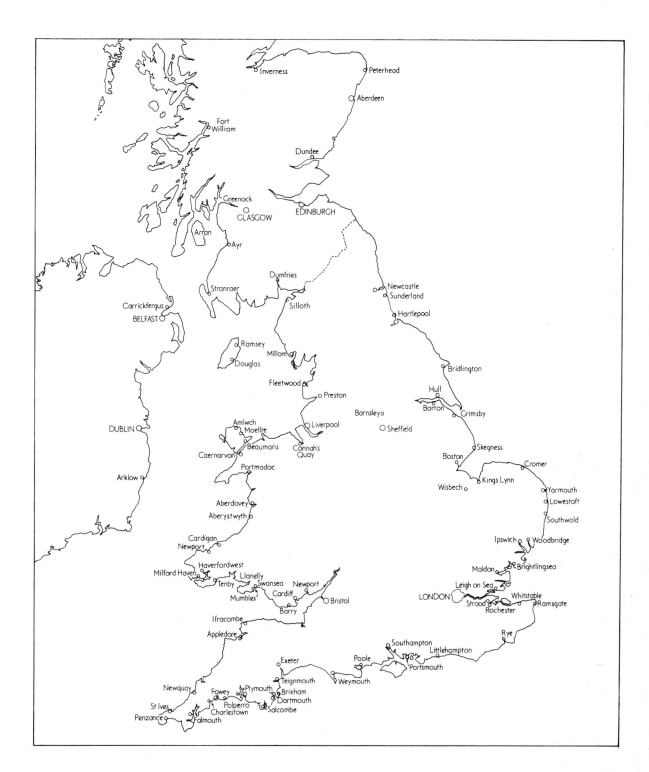

Inverness
Peterhead
Aberdeen
Fort William
Dundee
Greenock
GLASGOW
EDINBURGH
Arran
Ayr
Dumfries
Stranraer
Newcastle
Sunderland
Silloth
Hartlepool
Carrickfergus
BELFAST
Ramsey
Millom
Douglas
Bridlington
Fleetwood
Hull
Preston
Barton
Barnsley
Grimsby
Amlwch
Moelfre
Liverpool
DUBLIN
Sheffield
Beaumaris
Skegness
Caernarvon
Connah's Quay
Boston
Cromer
Portmadoc
Kings Lynn
Arklow
Wisbech
Yarmouth
Aberdovey
Lowestoft
Aberystwyth
Southwold
Cardigan
Ipswich
Woodbridge
Newport
Haverfordwest
Maldon
Brightlingsea
Milford Haven
Llanelly
Leigh on Sea
Tenby
Swansea
Newport
LONDON
Whitstable
Mumbles
Cardiff
Bristol
Strood
Ramsgate
Barry
Rochester
Ilfracombe
Appledore
Rye
Southampton
Littlehampton
Poole
Exeter
Portsmouth
Teignmouth
Weymouth
Newquay
Plymouth
Fowey
Brixham
St Ives
Polperro
Dartmouth
Penzance
Charlestown
Salcombe
Falmouth

Acknowledgements

For one person working on his own the gathering of the material in this book has been a gigantic and expensive task. It has been collected and researched over a period of about ten years during which time I have endeavoured to visit by land and sometimes sea all the places connected with traditional sailing vessels. This restless self-imposed pilgrimage has brought home to me not only how many ports, anchorages and landing places there are in the British Isles, but how completely different they all are. However, although there are many obvious differences, in Britain one can still move about freely without crossing any form of frontier.

In the West Country I have been helped by James Green, Terence Heard, Grahame Farr, Fiona Beale, Robin Selwood, Captain A.J. Martell, Pete Lucas and all those connected with *Charlotte Rhodes* and the *Marques*. In Wales two distinguished lifeboat coxwains, Dick Evans of Moelfre and Derek Scott of Mumbles, both spared me their time talking about sailing ships. So too did the Morris brothers at Newport, Pembrokeshire, and Mr L. J. Williams of Llangranog. Mr R.H.J. Lloyd, an authority on South Wales fishing boats, was most generous. Another local authority who was most helpful was Mr Alan Lockett of Barrow-in-Furness, and so too were Mr Trevor Morgan and Mr John Clarkson. Mr A.E. Truckell of the Dumfries Burgh Museum went to a great deal of trouble to aid this tribute to the Age of Sail.

As well as the people mentioned in the text those also helpful were Mr John Hainsworth and other members of the Humber Keel and Sloop Preservation Society and Mr Alan Robertson of the *Annie Maud* restoration project. On the East Coast Hugh Perks and Patricia O'Driscoll, editorial team of the *East Coast Digest* filled in some gaps. Thank you to R.J. Scott and ninety-two-year old Henry Harling for telling his memories of fishing off the coast of Suffolk; and also to Mr T.W. Belt, Mr Eric Stringer, Mr H. Brent, Mrs Dring and G.F. Cordy. Some material was given to me by Bill Coke and Robert More, who also crewed for me on my gaff cutter *L'Atalanta*. Collecting material on the past in a craft of that same period seems very appropriate.

Many of the photographs have come from my own collection or are ones I have taken. However I am most grateful to The Scott Polar Research Institute (Cambridge), Alexander Turnbull Library (Wellington), Manx Museum, Liverpool Public Libraries, Gwynedd Archives Service, National Library of Wales, Weymouth Museum of Local History, Poole Museums and the National Maritime Museum, Greenwich.

I would also like to thank John Lyman of California, the well known shipping magazine *Sea Breezes* and its editor, Craig J.M. Carter. Other published sources include material on the *Louisa Craig* by Jack Churchouse in the *Mariner's Mirror* and on the *Polly Woodside* by Graeme Robertson in the *Dog Watch*.

R.S.
Ramsholt

Index